KU-166-744

VEGAN GOODNESS

—

DELICIOUS PLANT-BASED RECIPES THAT CAN BE ENJOYED EVERY DAY

JESSICA PRESCOTT

VEGAN
GOODNESS

———

DELICIOUS PLANT-BASED RECIPES THAT
CAN BE ENJOYED EVERY DAY

from the creator of the blog *Wholy Goodness*

To Louie, my most delicious creation yet.

hardie grant books

CONTENTS

—

INTRODUCTION

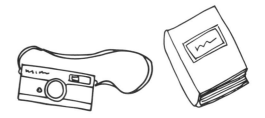

ABOUT ME

My earliest memories are in the kitchen with my mum, watching her bake, back when one of life's biggest joys was the moment she allowed me to lick the bowl. I was raised on home-cooked meals and my mum was revered amongst friends and family for her food – she was the one who always put on the best spread, who made everyone's birthday cakes, who discovered dukkah before it was trendy, and who embraced my decision to stop eating meat when I was 14 because she loved the inspiration my new diet brought into her kitchen. Needless to say, it is through my mum that I inherited my love for cooking. I've never had any professional training; I've simply been cooking for as long as I can remember. Little things my mum taught me have stuck – the rest I have picked up along the way, teaching myself as I go.

Growing up in a small town filled me with a wanderlust that has propelled me across the continents. I left Napier, New Zealand, when I was 17, and in every new city I've visited or lived in, I've gathered inspiration for what I can do with the humble vegetable. I now live in Berlin with my Australian husband, Andy, and my son Louie, who was growing inside me while I created this book.

My tiny Berlin kitchen is my happy place. I find cooking meditative and I relish the ritual of cooking for others because food has always been my way of connecting with people. My food is hearty and rustic as opposed to fancy and polished, with flavour being of utmost importance. For me, the best way to spend an evening is sharing food and wine out of mismatched plates and glasses with loved ones.

I am terrible at following recipes, but I love sharing my kitchen experiments with friends, which is what led me to start my blog *Wholy Goodness*. Initially, I wanted it to be a blog without photos, until a dear friend convinced me that these days, people need a photo to accompany a recipe. Little did I know, there was an amateur food stylist hiding inside me. When I was a child, I used to say that I would love to write a cookbook one day, but I never thought it would actually happen. Yet here I am. Writing the introduction for my first book, praying that I have managed to accurately record what I do in the kitchen and that between these pages anyone, from any part of the world, will find something that inspires them to occasionally make vegan choices.

WHY VEGAN?

—

I am vegan because to me, it is the lifestyle that makes the most sense for the wellbeing of this planet and every creature who inhabits it.

Not only is factory farming cruel, it is polluting the planet and using up its resources. The water and land that are being used to grow food for animals could instead be used to grow food for humans. This would reduce world hunger significantly.

And that's just the tip of the iceberg lettuce. But I am not writing a book to convince people to become vegan, I am writing a cookbook to show people how yummy vegan food can be. If you are wondering why more and more people are adopting this seemingly radical lifestyle, then I implore you to do your own research about factory farming and animal agriculture.

When your diet contains plentiful amounts of fruit, vegetables, nuts, seeds, legumes and grains, you are giving your body pure, clean energy that it knows exactly how to process, rather than filtering those nutrients through another being's body first.

I have a list of books, documentaries and websites that I have found helpful and informative on my blog, www.wholygoodness.com

FURTHER READING

Eating Animals, Jonathan Safran Foer (Little, Brown, 2009) – JSF had been swinging between vegetarian, vegan and omnivore diets for years and when his wife got pregnant, he decided to embark on a research project so that he could make sure that he raised his son on the best diet possible. What he found out was so compelling that he decided to publish it in a book. Be prepared to get mad.

DOCUMENTARIES

For your health – *Forks Over Knives,* Lee Fulkerson, 2011
For the planet – *Cowspiracy,* Kip Andersen and Keegan Kuhn, 2014
For the animals – *Earthlings,* Shaun Monson, 2005

MY VEGANISM

—

My own personal journey with veganism began when someone pointed out the moral dissonance of a vegetarian diet. At the time, I had no idea of the cruelty involved with dairy and egg farming. Every time a new documentary about veganism comes out I feel even more convinced that this is the right decision, but despite everything I know, the transition was not an overnight one for me.

A vegan diet makes the most sense for the health of humans, the wellbeing of animals and the future of our planet. But that doesn't mean the change is always easy. It requires preparation and a high level of dedication. I am lucky because I love to cook and I live in a vegan-friendly city, but there have certainly been times where I have found myself hangry and stranded in the middle of a city or village, with no vegan options in sight. From the beef fat in some potato fries to the milk powder in some types of breads, to the egg in noodles and the chicken stock used in soup, it can sometimes feel like there are animal products lurking in everything. These days I always carry nuts and dried fruit with me as a backup and I make sure to do my homework when travelling to new places, but it took me almost three years to reach this level of dedication.

A lot of people turn vegan overnight and never go back and I admire their commitment. But I feel that it is important to be transparent about my own journey so that people don't feel like they are failing if all their morals align with a vegan lifestyle but they 'slip up' every now and again. I eased myself into veganism by cooking only vegan food at home and making vegan choices when eating out, but making exceptions when travelling or when cheese was served with wine at a friend's house. When I decided to cook only vegan food, the realisation that I can make anything I want using plants and plant-based ingredients changed the way I cook. By removing animal products from my kitchen, I have discovered a whole new world of culinary possibilities using fruit, vegetables, nuts, seeds, legumes, grains and spices. Instead of doing what has always been done, I was forced to think outside the box. This is where my true creativity really set in and I found my niche as a vegan cook.

To me, every vegan meal that is eaten or cake that is baked is a victory. What I have shared in this book are dishes that I hope can be enjoyed by anyone – food that is so delicious, no one even notices the absence of meat. I want to dispel the myth about vegans and their food. Because no matter our dietary preferences, plants unite us all.

MY MANTRA

Sometimes, in low moments, when I realise that some people truly just don't care, my efforts can seem futile and I wonder if I am really even making a difference. But then I remember that I am doing this because I need to be the change I want to see. That's my mantra these days. And we all need a mantra or two...

... I hope that, even if you are the most carnivorous of omnivores, I have shown you how simple and delicious food can be, even without the meat, eggs and dairy, and that this inspires you to incorporate more plant-based meals into your day-to-day diet.

INCREDIBLE, EDIBLE EARTH!

—

I use ingredients that I find at my local produce market and organic supermarkets in Berlin. No tofu, no fake meat, no fake cheese – just things that grow from the earth. Every day I marvel over this incredible planet and the beautiful psychedelic and delicious things it grows. I mean, *look at a pomegranate, for crying out loud!* Every time I eat a grape I wonder why anyone would choose a bag of candy over a bunch of grapes. Regardless of whether you believe in evolution or the Bible, our blue planet, with its mountains, waterfalls, plants and animals, is truly a miracle that should not be taken for granted. We are so lucky to be here.

SHOPPING LIST

—

If you get into the habit of always having a few of your favourite vegetables on hand and a pantry full of beans, nuts, seeds, spices, condiments and your favourite grains or pastas, you will pretty much always be able to whip up something to eat. Your grocery haul will vary depending on where you live and your taste preferences, so let this list serve as a guide to be customised to your liking.

If you are new to cooking, don't be overwhelmed – especially not by the herbs and spices section. It took me two years of living in Berlin to build up my spice collection. It's best to start out slow and buy things as you need them, restocking the ones that you love so you don't waste money on ingredients that never get used.

FRESH

A few salady things, such as avocado, tomatoes, cucumber and carrots

Bananas – if you love smoothies, get into the habit of buying bananas every time you shop so that you always have some on hand

Flavour-makers, such as red onions, white onions, garlic and lemons

Herbs – I always have basil, parsley and coriander (cilantro) on hand and buy rosemary, thyme, and so on, as required

Leafy greens that you can eat raw, such as baby spinach or rocket (arugula)

Other veggies that you can cook in a pan for a quick meal such as aubergine (eggplant), courgette (zucchini) and mushrooms

Other seasonal greens, such as broccoli, kale, beans or brussels sprouts

Seasonal fruits – choose pomegranates, berries, figs, pears and stone fruits

Starchy rooty things, such as potatoes, sweet potatoes and pumpkin (squash)

LEGUMES

I like to have my favourites on hand, both dried and tinned, so I can whip up something in a pinch.

Black beans – nothing beats unsoaked black beans cooked from scratch with a bit of salt. Nothing. Use in anything Mexican-inspired, in burger patties or on their own with rice, or even in brownies!

Chickpeas – see An Ode to Chickpeas on page 18

Lentils – as a replacement for mincemeat in Italian recipes, in burger patties, in wraps, and so on

Split peas – lend a sweet and slightly smoky flavour to soups. Combined with celery and carrot, you have the base for a veggie soup that is guaranteed to be delicious

White beans – great in soups, stews, salads, dips, and mashed with garlic, lemon and herbs on toast as an alternative to eggs

STAPLES AND CONDIMENTS

Balsamic vinegar and **apple cider vinegar**

Coconut milk and your other favourite plant-based milks – I use rice milk quite a lot

Curry paste – green or red

Mustard – wholegrain or smooth

Olives – preferably with their stones in. They take longer to prepare, but their flavour is incomparable to pre-sliced olives

Peanut butter or any other nut butters you love

Pickled gherkins

Sea salt – including flakes

Sun-dried or **semi-dried tomatoes** – NOT the ones in oil

Syrup – something sweet such as maple syrup or date syrup

Tahini – a runny one and a thick one

Tamari or **soy sauce**

Tomato paste or **concentrated tomato purée** (the really thick stuff you find in tubes)

OILS

Avocado oil for high-heat cooking
Coconut oil for baking

Olive oil for salad dressings and pasta sauces

Sesame oil for Asian foods

NUTS, SEEDS AND DRIED FRUIT

Dried fruit – dates (both Medjool and Deglet Noor), figs and apricots, goji berries, cacao nibs

Nuts – almonds, cashew nuts, walnuts, hazelnuts, pine nuts

Seeds – sesame, sunflower, hemp, pumpkin, chia, flaxseeds

DRIED HERBS AND SPICES

Bay leaves

Black peppercorns

Cardamom*

Cinnamon*

Coriander*

Cumin*

Curry powder

Dried chilli

Garam masala

Ground ginger

Lovage

Mustard seeds

Nigella seeds

Nutmeg

Paprika (smoked if possible)

Sumac

Turmeric*

Vegetable stock

*I have whole and ground for each of these.

PASTA AND GRAINS

Your favourite **pasta noodles** – buy wholewheat. They are sooo much better for you and once you get used to them you will feel like they are giving you a hug from the inside when you eat them. If you find them a bit tough, just cook them for a little longer

Your favourite **grains** – wholegrain rice, quinoa, wholewheat couscous, freekeh, barley

BAKING

Baking powder and **bicarbonate of soda** (baking soda)

Brown Sugar such as raw demerara (turbinado) and muscavado. You can also use coconut sugar – just NOT white sugar!

Chocolate chips – preferably vegan

Cocoa

Coconut – both desiccated and flaked

Flour – preferably wholewheat but you can use plain (all-purpose) and buckwheat

Oats – quick and rolled

WEIRD INGREDIENTS

—

These are some things that you may not have heard of if you are new to vegan cooking. Once you get to know them they will become some of your favourite pantry essentials.

PSYLLIUM HUSK

The outer layer of the psyllium seed. Traditionally used to help with stomach trouble, it turns into a thick goo when mixed with water, making it a perfect substitute for eggs in vegan baking. You should be able to find it at your organic health food store or chemist – if not in the baking section, then in the 'medicine foods' section. Make psyllium husk your friend. Your insides will thank you for it.

HING

Also known as asafoetida, this STINKS! Walking around India you get whiffs of hing, but I never realised exactly what it was that I was smelling until the first time I bought my own little pot of this potent wonder herb. Its odour is so strong that I have to store it inside another jar to prevent it from stinking out my entire kitchen. But, once heated in oil, it provides a depth that my Indian cooking was always missing.

LIQUID SMOKE

Made by burning wood and collecting the smoke, which becomes a liquid as it cools. It is super strong and, when mixed with something sweet and something salty, lends a smoky flavour to cooking.

NUTRITIONAL YEAST

Nutritional yeast (also known as nooch) is a deactivated yeast. It is really good for you and a source of vitamin B12, which is the only vitamin that you can't obtain from plants. It is a little bit cheesy and I love to sprinkle it on top of pasta or avocado on toast, but you can also use it when blending nuts to make vegan cheese.

KITCHEN EQUIPMENT
I CAN'T LIVE WITHOUT

Kitchen tools and utensils do not have to be expensive to be functional. When I started my food blog I wanted to name it 'Ghetto Gourmet' because everything in my kitchen was second-hand, mismatched and ugly and I wanted to show people that you can make delicious food no matter how ghetto your kitchen setup is. All of this equipment can be found at a flea market, junk store or lurking in the back of your parents' kitchen cupboards. I repeat, fancy does not equal tasty.

GOOD KNIFE

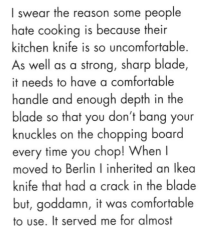

I swear the reason some people hate cooking is because their kitchen knife is so uncomfortable. As well as a strong, sharp blade, it needs to have a comfortable handle and enough depth in the blade so that you don't bang your knuckles on the chopping board every time you chop! When I moved to Berlin I inherited an Ikea knife that had a crack in the blade but, goddamn, it was comfortable to use. It served me for almost three years before I got a fancy one for my 30th birthday.

WOODEN
CHOPPING BOARD

One or a few. Wood is best because it won't blunt your knife blades like plastic and glass, but it will absorb flavours, so either keep separate ones for fruit and veg or wash immediately after chopping onions and garlic.

SILICONE SPATULA

These things are a dream!!! I use mine for everything – you'll be amazed by how much hummus or pesto is hiding in plain sight on the sides of the food processor or how much extra smoothie you can get by scraping the walls of your blender.

TABLESPOON
WITH A COMFY HANDLE

Possibly the most underrated tool in the kitchen, but if your spoon has a sharp square handle instead of a comfortable rounded one, it is going to make scraping out the seeds from a pumpkin, smoothing the top of brownie batter or nut roast, smearing hummus onto a wrap, stirring porridge, spooning chia pudding, and all the other tasks that you will use it for, a whole lot less comfortable.

COOKING EQUIPMENT

Blender or immersion blender – for soups, smoothies, burger patties etc.

Cake tins – long tin: 28 cm (11 in) round springform tins:18 cm (7 in) and 23 cm (9 in)

Colander/sieve

Food processor – so damn awesome when you make as much hummus as I do. I bought a new one after I killed my second-hand food processor trying to chop nuts for a nut roast. I've never looked back

Frying pan (skillet)

Grater – a box grater with a microplane to get the rind off your citrus fruits

Lasagne dish – also good for baking

brownies in

Lemon juicer

Measuring cups – and spoons if
you prefer your kitchen undertakings
to be precise

Serrated bread knife – use this
to cut tomatoes too

Slotted spoon

Soup ladle

Small, medium and large saucepans

Spiralizer (zoodle maker) – to make
courgette (zucchini) and carrot
noodles. Totally not essential,
but worth the money if you are
gluten-free or love pasta but
want to cut down on
the carbs

Stainless steel spatula

Tin (can) opener

Various baking trays

Vegetable brush

Vegetable peeler

Whisk

Wooden spoon

TIPS AND TRICKS

—

SLOW DOWN

Whether you're an accomplished cook or a beginner, sloooow down. Take a minute. Read the recipe. Get all your ingredients in one place. Put on some music or a podcast. Pour yourself a big glass of water. Drink it and then pour yourself another (or a wine). Do the dishes or at least clear enough space to cook in and make sure all the equipment you need is clean. It feels like more effort in the beginning, especially when you're hungry and you just wanna make your damn meal, but slowing down for a minute and getting your space and mind organised will make the whole process much smoother and more efficient in the long run. And remember to breathe. I have to remember this too sometimes. When I'm hungry and rushing I find myself taking shallow breaths instead of deep belly ones. The kitchen should not be stressful. It should be your happy place.

AN ODE TO CHICKPEAS

How do I love chickpeas? Let me count the ways…

— In curries instead of chicken
— In sandwiches instead of eggs
— As falafels, hummus, croutons
— In salads, sprouted, ground into flour and turned into savoury pancakes…

Seriously, there are so many possibilities with these little legumes of goodness I could write a book full of chickpea recipes. Plus, they are really, really good for you.

Get into the habit of cooking a bag of them every Sunday. You can then store them in the fridge for up to 1 week or freeze them if you don't think you will get through them all.

GRINDING FLAXSEEDS

It really is best to buy whole flaxseeds, especially when baking, as pre-ground flaxseeds can go rancid and ruin the taste of an entire cake. If you use your food processor to grind your seeds and find that they fly everywhere, put a little water in the blending vessel with the seeds, then grind. Or use a coffee grinder (much easier!), if you have one.

WASH YOUR VEGGIES AS SOON AS YOU GET THEM HOME

This way, everything is ready to rock and roll as soon as you feel like cooking. This is especially important for herbs, as nothing is worse than chopping soggy wet herbs (except biting into a piece of sand that is stuck to an unwashed herb). I haven't started every recipe with this because I'm gonna assume you are doing it. For herbs and leafy greens, I like to fill the sink and then submerge the greens for at least five minutes to make sure all the sandy, silty dirt comes away. Then dry in a colander.

COOKING
WITHOUT A RECIPE

—

All recipes aside, my favourite thing to do is chuck
some mushrooms in a pan with a handful of cooked
beans or lentils, sometimes some aubergine (eggplant)
or courgette (zucchini), let it all cook until it's mushy,
then serve it with some salady things in a bowl or in
a wrap. In fact, I eat a variation of exactly that at least
once a day. I also love to roast a whole lotta veggies
and smother them in tahini and pomegranate seeds,
storing leftovers in the fridge for salads and sandwiches
over the days that follow. Roasted vegetables and
avocado are a match made in heaven, as are baked
potatoes with hummus and coleslaw.

Another way to make a yummy meal without
following a recipe is to cook a grain of your choice,
top it with lots of fresh veggies, some herbs, nuts or
chickpeas, and eat!

QUICK EATS

—

Kale Scones 22
Quick Nachos 25
Pasta Salad 26
Curried Chickpea Salad Sanga 29
Tabbouleh 31
Sweetcorn Fritters 32

KALE SCONES

—

This is my spin on a savoury scone. Like all scones, they are best eaten straight out of the oven, smothered in some kind of dip or dunked into a soup or stew.

YOU NEED TO...

Preheat the oven to 180°C (350°F/Gas 4) and place the shelf on the middle rack.

Place a frying pan (skillet) on a medium heat and cover the bottom with a thin layer of olive oil. Cut the onions in quarters to remove the skin, then cut each quarter into 5 mm (¼ in) slices. Place in the pan and stir for a couple of minutes.

Rinse the kale leaves. Slice down the middle, removing the toughest part of the stem, then slice each leaf into 5 mm (¼ in) strips. Add to the pan with the onions. Stir until the onions are translucent and the kale is limp. Remove from the heat.

Place the flour, baking powder and salt in a large mixing bowl and stir with a fork to combine. Add the olive oil and stir again with the fork, then use your fingers to mix thoroughly. Add the nut milk, then using the fork followed by your fingers, gently combine everything together. Add the kale and onion mixture and use your hands to again, gently combine the dough.

Still using your hands, place 8 blobs of scone mix onto an oiled baking tray. Sprinkle the scones with pumpkin or sesame seeds and additional salt if you're a salty lady like me. Bake for 10–12 minutes or until golden. Remove and allow to cool for 10 minutes before eating.

CH-CH-CH-CH-CHANGES...

If you can't find kale, use spinach or chard leaves.

SHOPPING LIST

a drizzle of olive oil, for the pan
2 small white onions, peeled
4–6 large kale leaves

For the scone mixture:
375 g (13 oz/3 cups) plain (all-purpose) flour
6 teaspoons baking powder
1 teaspoon sea salt
50 ml (2 fl oz/¼ cup) olive oil
250 ml (8½ fl oz/1 cup) nut milk of your choice
pumpkin or sesame seeds, to garnish
sea salt flakes, to garnish (optional)

QUICK NACHOS

Legend has it that nachos were invented during World War Two, when a group of women entered a Mexican restaurant after they had already closed for the day. Not wanting them to go hungry, the head waiter whipped them up a snack with what little supplies he could find in the kitchen – tortillas, cheese and jalapeños. So delicious was his improvised creation that a new Tex-Mex staple was born – the beloved nachos, named after their creator, Ingacio 'Nacho' Anaya.

These are so different from the original that I'm sure purists would argue over their authenticity, but dammit they are delicious. In my home, these are a year-round classic, but if you eat them only once, be sure to do so on October 21st, the International Day of the Nacho.

YOU NEED TO...

Preheat the oven to 160°C (325°F/Gas 3).

Place the tortilla chips in a heatproof oven dish. Drain the beans and sprinkle these on top of the chips.

Make your salsa according to the recipe on page 83. About halfway through the process, your oven will be hot and ready. At this point, place the tortilla chips and beans in the oven and then finish making your salsa.

Remove the now-warm tortilla chips and beans from the oven (use a tea towel or oven mitt). Stir the salsa so everything is just combined and then dollop it over the warm beans.

Drizzle over the Cashew Cream, top with the avocado and chillies and squeeze over the lime juice. Sprinkle with any extra toppings of your choice such as pomegranate seeds or diced mango. Eat!

ON A HOT SUMMER NIGHT...

... skip the heating step and build these cold, kind of like a nacho salad!

SHOPPING LIST

2–4 large handfuls of tortilla (corn) chips

1 tin black beans or 250 g (9 oz/1½ cups) cooked black beans

Chunky Mexi-Corn Salsa (see page 83)

Cashew Cream (see page 140)

1 medium ripe avocado, chopped into cubes

1–2 small chillies (of your choice), finely chopped

1 lime, sliced, to dress

Optional extras:
a handful of pomegranate seeds

mango chunks

pineapple chunks

jalapeños

lettuce

vegan cheese (sprinkled on top of the beans before placing in the oven)

VEGAN GOODNESS

PASTA SALAD

——

Delicious hot or cold, this is something I could eat every night, if my thighs allowed it...

YOU NEED TO...

Cook the pasta according to the directions on the packet. Once the pasta is cooked, drain and then immerse in cold water to prevent it from cooking any further. Strain once cooled. This is an important step, otherwise you will find your pasta pieces stick together and become mushy.

Thinly slice the mushrooms and asparagus and cook in a little olive oil for 5 minutes, until the mushrooms have softened. The asparagus should still have a little crunch.

Stir the pesto through the pasta so that it is evenly coated, then add in the cooked mushrooms and asparagus plus all the remaining ingredients. Garnish with the pistachios before serving.

Eat immediately or store in the fridge for up to 2 days.

SOMETHING I LEARNT

If you make this using buckwheat pasta, you've really gotta eat it immediately. Otherwise it will become one big clump of buckwheat. And it doesn't taste good.

SHOPPING LIST

500 g (1 lb 2 oz/5½ cups) pasta, such as penne, orecchiette, shells, spirals

200 g (7 oz) brown mushrooms

1 bunch of asparagus (about 6–7 spears)

olive oil

3–4 tablespoons Green Pesto (see page 136)

10 cherry tomatoes, halved or quartered

2–3 handfuls of rocket (arugula) or baby spinach

½ medium red onion, peeled and very finely sliced

4 tablespoons toasted pistachio, or flaked almonds, to garnish

Optional extras:
olives
artichoke hearts
spring onions (scallions)

CURRIED CHICKPEA SALAD SANGA

———

I used to miss my dad's curried egg sandwiches until the guys at *Thug Kitchen* gave me the idea of using chickpeas in place of eggs in my sandwich. This is yet another wonderful way to use my beloved chickpeas!

YOU NEED TO...

Drain and rinse the chickpeas and place in a medium-sized bowl with the avocado, olive oil and lemon juice. Mash with a fork until well combined but still a little bit chunky.

Finely chop the onion, pickles and parsley and add to the chickpea mix along with the curry powder and salt and pepper. Stir to combine. Taste. Add more salt or curry powder if necessary.

You don't need me to tell you how to build the sandwich: bread, lettuce, chickpea salad, bread, squish it down, stuff it in your mouth.

SHOPPING LIST

For the curried chickpea salad:
250 g (9 oz/1½ cups) cooked chickpeas or 1 tin
1 large ripe avocado, chopped
a drizzle of olive oil
a squeeze of fresh lemon
1 small red onion, peeled
4 dill pickles
a handful of parsley leaves
1 tablespoon curry powder
sea salt and freshly ground black pepper

For the sandwich:
4 rolls or 8 slices of bread
baby butterhead lettuce (or any lettuce of your choice) or baby spinach

TABBOULEH

——

A version of the Middle Eastern classic that is hearty enough to be enjoyed on its own or as an accompaniment to an infinite number of dishes.

YOU NEED TO...

Cook your grain according to the directions on the packet. While the grain is cooking, place the cumin seeds and pine nuts in a frying pan over a medium heat and toast, stirring frequently, until fragrant and lightly browned. Remove from the heat and set aside.

Finely chop the onion, tomatoes, cucumber and radishes and place in a large bowl with the chickpeas. Finely chop the mint and parsley leaves and add to the bowl. You can leave the fine stalks that join the parsley leaves to the stalk, but remove any strong stalky bits so they don't poke you in the mouth when you are eating.

When your grain has finished cooking, allow to cool slightly and then pour a splash of olive oil over it and sprinkle with some salt. Fluff the grain with a fork so that the pieces are separated and there are no clumps. Add the grain to the bowl and stir to combine with the herbs and veggies.

Dress with lemon juice and some freshly ground black pepper and stir again, then top with the toasted cumin seeds and pine nuts. Sprinkle over the pomegranate seeds and serve immediately or store in the fridge for up to 3 days.

CH-CH-CH-CH-CHANGES...

This recipe is incredibly versatile and there are a million variations. Try spring onions (scallions), chives, basil or coriander (cilantro) for a slightly different flavour. Leave out the radishes or cucumber if you dislike them and experiment with different grains. Toasted, flaked almonds are incredibly delicious sprinkled on top. Chopped avocado works well too.

SHOPPING LIST

175 g (6 oz/1 cup) of a grain of your choice; traditionally burghul (bulgur) is used but you can use couscous, quinoa, freekeh, millet or even cauliflower rice

1 tablespoon cumin seeds

2 tablespoons pine nuts

1 small red onion, peeled

3 large red tomatoes or 2 handfuls of cherry tomatoes

1 small cucumber

6 small red radishes

50–250 g (3–9 oz/½–1½ cups) cooked chickpeas or ⅓–1 tin, drained and rinsed

a handful of mint leaves

3 handfuls of flat-leaf (Italian) parsley

olive oil

sea salt, to taste

juice of 1 lemon

freshly ground black pepper, to taste

seeds of ½ pomegranate, to garnish

SWEETCORN FRITTERS

A childhood staple – veganised.

YOU NEED TO...

If using tinned sweetcorn, squeeze all of the water out of the corn before using – I usually open the tin, pour it into a colander and leave while I prep the other ingredients, then squeeze any leftover water out with my hands. This will make a HUGE difference to the taste and texture of your fritters.

Place a cast-iron or non-stick frying pan (skillet) on a medium–high heat. Whisk together the flour, bicarbonate of soda, salt, freshly ground black pepper and rice or soya milk. Mix in the chopped red onion, coriander and diced pepper to the the batter. Add the corn and mix together until fully combined. It will seem like you don't have enough batter. This is good. You want just enough to glue the other ingredients together, no more.

Pour enough oil into the pan to lightly coat the bottom. Spoon tablespoons of the batter into a frying pan. I usually do three at a time so that there is room to flip them. Flatten them ever so slightly with the back of the tablespoon so that they don't break when you flip them and they can cook through evenly.

When bubbles appear, flip and allow to cook for an additional 2–3 minutes or until golden brown. Repeat until all of the batter is used up.

My favourite way to eat these is piled into a sandwich (as pictured), with my Classic Hummus, Caramelised Onions, fresh coriander, guacamole and whatever other goodies I have in my fridge.

CH-CH-CH-CH-CHANGES...

Use buckwheat, rice or besan (chickpea flour) in place of wholemeal flour. If you are missing the tang that feta usually lends to such fritters, try adding a few chopped sun-dried tomatoes or pitted, chopped green olives.

SHOPPING LIST

400 g (14 oz/2 cups) tinned sweetcorn (corn kernels) or kernels from 3 cobs

125 g (4 oz/1 cup) wholemeal plain (all-purpose) flour

½ teaspoon bicarbonate of soda (baking soda)

½ teaspoon sea salt

150 ml (5 fl oz/½ cup) rice or soy milk

1 small red onion, peeled and finely chopped

a small handful of coriander (cilantro) stalks (optional), finely chopped

1 red (bell) pepper, diced

vegetable oil, for frying

To serve as a sandwich (optional):

slices of crusty bread

Classic Hummus (see page 92)

Caramelised Onions (see page 149)

a handful of coriander (cilantro)

guacamole

ONE-HOUR MEALS

—

Spag Bol with Courgette Zoodles 36
Black Rice Salad 39
Jackfruit Tacos 40
Mushroom Stew 43
Spinach and Chickpea Curry 44
Thai Green Curry 47
Golden Soup with Chickpea Croutons 48
Potato, Leek and White Bean Soup 51
Summer Roll Salad 52
Black Bean Burgers 54

SPAG BOL WITH COURGETTE ZOODLES

Replacing minced meat with lentils is one of the easiest swaps when you want to reduce or remove the meat in your diet. Here is a recipe for Bolognese that does exactly that. If you have time, make it in advance as it is always outrageously good the day after making.

YOU NEED TO...

If using dried lentils, cook them in 500 ml (17 fl oz/2 cups) of water for 20 minutes.

Make the tomato sauce according to the recipe on page 138. Finely chop the sun-dried tomatoes and mushrooms and add these to the sauce as you are cooking, along with the balsamic vinegar.

When the lentils are cooked, drain and add these or the tinned lentils to the sauce and allow to simmer for an additional 10 minutes or until you are ready to serve.

Transform your courgettes into zoodles using a spiralizer and lightly blanch them in boiling water, if you like. If you prefer them raw, place them straight on the plate. Top the zoodles with the sauce and sprinkle with the pumpkin seeds and basil leaves.

Serve with crusty bread to undo all the goodness of eating courgette noodles instead of wheat noodles!

CH-CH-CH-CH-CHANGES...

If you don't own a spiralizer you can use normal spaghetti or any other pasta your heart desires. You can also make sloppy joes and serve the sauce on buns instead of noodles, if you prefer.

SHOPPING LIST

185 g (6½ oz/1 cup) dried green or brown lentils (I prefer Puy) or 2 tins, drained

1 portion of Fresh Tomato Napoli Sauce (see page 138)

a small handful of sun-dried tomatoes (not the ones in oil)

500 g (1 lb 2 oz) mushrooms of your choice

1 tablespoon balsamic vinegar

4 medium courgettes (zucchini)

toasted pumpkin seeds and basil, to serve

BLACK RICE SALAD

Perfect to take along to a potluck or to enjoy as a dinner, followed by a leftovers lunch the next day.

YOU NEED TO...

First cook the rice. Put the rice and 500 ml (17 fl oz/2 cups) of water in a medium-sized saucepan. Bring to the boil and then lower to a simmer for 40 minutes. Remove from the heat, stir in the oil and allow to cool a little while you prepare the other ingredients.

Finely dice the red onion, cherry tomatoes and pepper. Thinly slice the radish and chilli, if using. Roughly chop the greens, slice the avocado, remove the seeds from the pomegranate and juice the lime. Toast the cumin seeds and pine nuts together in a pan over a medium heat until just fragrant.

Place the fresh ingredients in the pan with the cooked black rice and stir to combine. Serve with a sprinkling of the toasted cumin seeds and pine nuts. If you are not serving this right away, make sure the rice is completely cool before adding the fresh ingredients so that the heat of the rice doesn't cause them to wilt.

CH-CH-CH-CH-CHANGES...

As always, this is one of those dishes that you can customise depending on what you have on hand. Pineapple is a great substitue for pomegranate and flaked almonds work just as well as pine nuts.

SHOPPING LIST

200 g (7 oz/1 cup) black rice

3 tablespoons avocado or olive oil

1 medium red onion, peeled

2–3 large handfuls of cherry tomatoes

1 yellow (bell) pepper

1 long red radish or 6 round red radishes

1 red chilli (optional)

2 large handfuls of baby spinach or other salad greens

a large handful each of parsley and coriander (cilantro)

1 large ripe avocado

½ pomegranate

1 lime

1 tablespoon cumin seeds

3 tablespoons pine nuts

JACKFRUIT TACOS

This is one of those things that you won't believe until you try it. Once cooked, the texture of the jackfruit is so meat-like, I have had friends worriedly ask, 'is that vegetarian?' when serving it at barbecues. You can buy jackfruit at any good Asian supermarket, but it's important you get the baby jackfruit in brine, not the type in syrup.

YOU NEED TO...

Heat a little oil over a medium heat in the bottom of a saucepan and add the finely chopped onion. Stir until transparent.

Add the cinnamon and cumin and stir until fragrant, then add the tomatoes, tomato paste, liquid smoke (if using), paprika, sugar, garlic and apple cider vinegar.

Drain the jackfruit and add this to the sauce once it's simmering. Allow to simmer while you prep the salsa and other toppings, stirring occasionally.

After half an hour the jackfruit should be very tender and you will be able to separate it out with your wooden spoon, tongs or a fork. Do this and stir together once more so that all of the jackfruit pieces are evenly coated in sauce.

Build the tacos: jackfruit, salsa, avocado, Cashew Cream, pomegranate, lime juice and slices of chilli.

CH-CH-CH-CH-CHANGES...

If you don't have all of the ingredients to make this from scratch, it is also delicious if you cook the jackfruit in a store-bought barbecue sauce. Serve it with my Coleslaw (see page 82) for a match made in heaven.

If you can't find jackfruit in brine, this same method can be used with seitan, tempeh, tofu or mushrooms.

SHOPPING LIST

olive oil

1 medium red or white onion, peeled and finely chopped

½ teaspoon ground cinnamon

1 teaspoon cumin seeds

400 g (14 oz) tin chopped tomatoes

2 tablespoons tomato paste (concentrated purée)

1 teaspoon liquid smoke (see page 15), (optional but awesome)

1 teaspoon smoked paprika

1 tablespoon brown sugar

3 garlic cloves, peeled and crushed

1 teaspoon apple cider vinegar

565 g (20 oz) tin jackfruit in brine

For the tacos:

8 taco shells

Chunky Mexi-Corn Salsa (see page 83)

1 large ripe avocado, mashed

Cashew Cream (see page 140)

seeds of ½ pomegranate

1 lime, quartered, to serve

1 large green chilli, sliced

MUSHROOM STEW

Part soup, part casserole, this hearty mushroom stew is my favourite way to celebrate the cooling autumn weather.

YOU NEED TO...

Put a saucepan over a medium heat and add enough oil to lightly cover the bottom.

Finely chop half of the mushrooms. Add these with the chopped onions and tomatoes to the pan and stir. Chunkily chop the remaining mushrooms and drop them into the pan.

Stir in the garlic, along with the veggie stock, nutmeg, flour, paprika, thyme and freshly ground black pepper. Mix it well and make sure there are no lumps of flour floating around. It should have thickened a little. If not, add a little more flour.

Add the bay leaves and allow to simmer for half an hour. Taste and add salt as necessary. I find my veggie stock salty enough, but if you are using a low-sodium brand you may need to add some salt to bring out the flavour. Stir through the chopped parsely just before serving.

Eat this with mashed potato (see the Masala Mash recipe on page 97, swapping out the spices for some fresh herbs such as chives or rosemary), quinoa, crusty bread and whatever green veggies you have on hand, such as kale, spinach or broccoli.

SHOPPING LIST

olive oil

1 kg (2 lb 3 oz) assorted mushrooms

1 large white onion, peeled and finely chopped

3 tomatoes, finely chopped

4 garlic cloves, peeled and finely chopped

1 litre (34 fl oz/4 cups) vegetable stock

½ teaspoon ground nutmeg

2–4 tablespoons plain (all-purpose) flour (you can use wholemeal or a gluten-free variety such as rice flour)

1 teaspoon each of smoked paprika and dried thyme (optional)

freshly ground black pepper

2 bay leaves

sea salt (optional)

a large handful of flat-leaf (Italian) parsley, finely chopped

To serve (optional):

mashed potato, quinoa or crusty bread and whatever greens you have in your fridge

SPINACH AND CHICKPEA CURRY

A rich Indian curry for when you are in need of a green fix.

YOU NEED TO...

Cook the rice according to your preferred cooking method or prepare the Masala Mash as per the recipe on page 97.

Bring a large saucepan of water to the boil. Place the spinach in the water and cook for 3 minutes. Drain and then purée with the ginger and half of the crushed garlic. Some people recommend placing the spinach in an ice bath after blanching, so that it retains its colour. You can do this if you like, but it is not necessary.

Dry the saucepan in which you blanched the spinach, and place it back on a medium heat. Melt the coconut oil in the pan and add the finely chopped onions and cumin seeds. Stir for a couple of minutes and then add the remaining garlic and tomatoes.

Cook until the tomatoes are soft and then add the turmeric, garam masala, hing and salt. Stir for a minute and then add the spinach purée and about 400 ml (14 fl oz/¾ cups) of water. Gently stir a little more and then add the chickpeas and coconut milk. Place the lid on the pan and allow to simmer for 20 minutes or for up to 2 hours if you are making it in advance.

Serve with the basmati rice or Masala Mash and garnish with cashews, coriander and an extra splash of coconut milk.

SHOPPING LIST

400 g (12 oz/2 cups) basmati rice or Masala Mash (see page 97)

500 g (1 lb 2 oz) baby spinach

2.5 cm (1 in) piece of fresh ginger

5 garlic cloves, peeled and crushed

1 large tablespoon coconut oil

1 medium white onion, peeled and finely chopped

2 teaspoons cumin seeds

4 small tomatoes, chopped

1 teaspoon ground turmeric

2 teaspoons garam masala

¼ teaspoon hing (asafoetida)

1 teaspoon sea salt

2 tins of cooked chickpeas or 500 g (1lb 2 oz/3 cups)

1–2 tablespoons coconut milk, plus extra to serve

a hanful of cashews, to garnish

a handful of coriander (cilantro), finely chopped, to garnish

THAI GREEN CURRY

Thai curries are one of my favourite ways to introduce meat eaters to vegan cooking. By simply swapping the meat for chickpeas, a Thai green curry becomes accidentally vegan.

YOU NEED TO...

Cook the rice according to your preferred cooking method.

Drain and rinse your chickpeas and chop your hard and starchy vegetable, removing the skin if it's a hard-skinned pumpkin (I leave the skin on if using potatoes, sweet potatoes or Hokkaido pumpkin).

Heat the coconut oil in a large saucepan over a medium heat. Add the onion, garlic and coriander stalks (reserve the leaves) and stir until the onion is soft and translucent. Add the curry paste and stir until fragrant.

Add the coconut milk, chickpeas and pumpkin and increase the heat to high. Once boiling, add the mushrooms and aubergine, then lower the heat and allow to simmer for about 30 minutes, until the starchy vegetable and aubergine are easily pierced with a fork. Add the sugar snap peas right before serving.

Spoon the cooked rice into 4 bowls, top with the curry and garnish with the reserved coriander leaves, coconut flakes and chillies.

CH-CH-CH-CH-CHANGES...

You can use tofu or tempeh in place of the chickpeas if you like. Use red or yellow curry paste instead of green. Replace half of the coconut milk with water if you are worried about fat, but keep in mind that coconut milk is very, very good for you and full of 'good fats' (the ones your body knows how to process). Feel free to add any any extra vegetables you like, such as broccoli, cauliflower, bean sprouts, courgette (zucchini) and (bell) pepper.

SHOPPING LIST

400 g (12 oz/2 cups) brown jasmine rice

250 g (9 oz/1½ cups) cooked chickpeas or 1 tin

1 large starchy veggie like a pumpkin (squash), sweet potato or normal potatoes

2 tablespoons coconut oil

1 large white onion, peeled and finely chopped

3 garlic cloves, peeled and finely chopped

a bunch of coriander (cilantro), stalks and leaves separated, and stalks finely chopped

green curry paste for 4 people (you will need to check the packet but this is usually 1–2 tablespoons)

500 ml (17 fl oz/2 cups) coconut milk

1–2 handfuls of brown mushrooms, sliced

1 small aubergine (eggplant), chopped into cubes

1–2 handfuls of sugar snap peas

coconut flakes, to garnish

red chillies, sliced, to garnish

GOLDEN SOUP WITH CHICKPEA CROUTONS

——

A cool-weather soup to make you shine from the inside out.

YOU NEED TO...

Preheat the oven to 180°C (350°F/Gas 4).

To make the croutons, rinse and drain the chickpeas. Place in a saucepan with the oil, spices and salt, add a lid and shake so they are all coated in deliciousness. Pour into a roasting dish and cook for 30–40 minutes.

To make the soup, peel and roughly chop the onion, ginger and turmeric (if using fresh) and set aside.

Chop the orange veggies into approximately 1.5 cm (½ in) cubes. I leave the skin on everything I can, but if you are using a pumpkin with a tough skin (i.e. anything that's not Hokkaido), you will need to remove the skin before cooking.

Pour enough oil into a saucepan to cover the base and place the pan on a medium heat. Add the chopped onion, ginger and turmeric to the pan. Stir with a wooden spoon for a couple of minutes and then add the chopped orange vegetables.

Pour in the vegetable stock, then add the chopped garlic with the bay leaf and spices. Season with some freshly ground black pepper then place the lid on top. Bring to the boil and then lower to a simmer, stirring occasionally to ensure nothing is sticking to the bottom of the pan.

SHOPPING LIST

....

For the croutons:

250 g (9 oz/1½ cups) cooked chickpeas or 1 tin

2 tablespoons olive oil

½ teaspoon ground turmeric

1 teaspoon ground cumin

½ teaspoon garlic powder (optional but really, really yummy)

1 teaspoon sea salt

For the soup:

1 medium onion (about 125 g/4 oz/ ¾ cup when chopped)

1 thumb-sized piece of fresh ginger

1 thumb-sized piece of fresh turmeric or 1 teaspoon ground turmeric

1 large sweet potato*

3 medium carrots*

½ medium pumpkin or squash*

olive oil

1 litre (34 fl oz/4 cups) vegetable stock or 1 teaspoon lovage and 1 teaspoon sea salt mixed into 1 litre (34 fl oz/4 cups) water

4 garlic cloves, peeled and chopped

1 bay leaf

1 teaspoon ground coriander (optional)

½ teaspoon cayenne pepper

freshly ground black pepper, to taste

* you need about 500 g (1 lb 2 oz) of each orange vegetable, once chopped, or about 1.5 kg (3 lb 5 oz) in total, but don't stress over quantities

Cook for approximately 30 minutes or until the veggies are easily mushed when pressed with the back of the spoon. When cooked, allow to cool for 10 minutes, remove the bay leaf and blend the soup until smooth.

Serve in bowls, topped with the chickpea croutons and your choice of fresh herbs, pesto, or a yummy oil such as olive, avocado, pumpkin seed or walnut. Eat with my savoury Kale Scones (see page 22) or some warm crusty bread.

POTATO, LEEK AND WHITE BEAN SOUP

Potato and leek soup is one of my all-time favourite soups, flavour-wise, but as a meal it is a bit lacking nutritionally. In order to be able to justify eating it as a meal I add white beans, which boost the protein and iron content while making this a soup that actually keeps you full.

YOU NEED TO...

Place a little oil in the bottom of a pan and then place over a medium heat. Chop the onions, garlic, leeks and potatoes, adding to the pan as you go and stirring after each addition.

Add the beans, veggie stock, bay leaf and salt. Bring the soup to the boil and then lower to a simmer. Allow to simmer for 20 minutes or until the potatoes are easily pierced with a fork.

Remove from the heat and allow to cool for 10 minutes. Remove the bay leaf and blend the soup until smooth.

Serve topped with lots of black pepper, fresh herbs of your choice, chilli and toasted bread. Carbs on carbs on carbs. Yum.

HOT TIP

If you prefer a chunkier soup, only blend half of the soup and then stir the remaining chunks through.

SHOPPING LIST

olive oil

2 large white onions, peeled

4 garlic cloves, peeled

3 leeks

1 kg (2 lb 3 oz) large potatoes, scrubbed and washed

500 g (1 lb 2 oz/3 cups) cooked white beans or 2 tins, drained

1.5 litres (2½ pints) vegetable stock

1 bay leaf

2 teaspoons sea salt

freshly ground black pepper, to taste

herbs, such as parsley, chives or winter savory

crushed red chilli, to taste

toasted bread, to serve

SUMMER ROLL SALAD

—

You know when you feel like eating summer rolls but you can't be bothered with all that prep and all that rolling? This is my solution.

YOU NEED TO...

Cook the noodles according to the packet directions and then drizzle with a little sesame oil to prevent them from sticking.

Slice the carrots and red pepper into fine matchsticks. Thinly slice the radishes, cucumbers and avocado. Roughly chop the herbs. Place all the ingredients in a bowl, pour the dressing over the top and use your hands to combine everything together.

Chop the spring onions and sprinkle these on top along with the nuts and sesame seeds. Serve immediately!

CH-CH-CH-CH-CHANGES...

I know herbs can be expensive, so if you can't do all three, add some baby spinach for bulk and just use whatever herbs you can.

SHOPPING LIST

rice noodles for 4 people (about 2 packets or 300 g /10½ oz)

a drizzle of toasted sesame oil

3 medium carrots, peeled

1 medium red (bell) pepper

a handful of radishes

1 large or 3 baby cucumbers

1 large ripe avocado

1–2 large handfuls each of coriander (cilantro), mint and Thai basil

Maple Lime Dressing (see page 146)

2–5 spring onions (scallions)

1–2 large handfuls of cashew nuts or peanuts

black sesame seeds, to garnish

© AINO-MAIJA METSOLA 201

BLACK BEAN BURGERS

Who doesn't love a burger? This recipe is so simple and delicious, it's loved by vegans, anyone on a gluten-free diet, and meat-eaters alike.

One burger is definitely enough to fill a belly, but I like to serve these with Yuca Fries (see page 96) or a side salad, especially when hosting guests, as dinner parties are about pigging out, right??

YOU NEED TO...

Pour a little bit of oil in the bottom of a medium-sized saucepan and place this over a medium heat. Add the cumin seeds, onion and garlic and stir until the onion begins to go transparent.

Add most of but NOT ALL of the black beans (I like to save about a third). Stir for a few minutes until the beans are nice and soft and then remove from the heat and mash into a smooth paste.

Stir in the oats or flour, salt, paprika and some freshly ground black pepper into the blended bean mix. Add the remaining beans and the corn and coriander, then use your hands to combine everything. At this point you should be able to form patties. If the mixture is still a little wet, add more oats or flour, a tablespoon at a time. If it is a little dry, add some water or oil.

Place a heavy-bottomed frying pan on a medium–high heat. Form your mixture into 4 large or 6 medium patties and cook in the hot pan until golden brown or lightly blackened, depending on your taste preferences.

Prepare the other burger ingredients while your patties cook – toast your buns or wash your lettuce leaves, slice the tomato, onion and avocado (or mash it into guacamole), pick the leaves of your coriander and make the Chipotle Mayo. Now you can build your burger from bottom to top as follows: bun (or lettuce leaf), avocado, patty, tomato, onion, coriander, mayo, lid. And then figure out how to get your mouth around it. Serve with a large portion of Yuca Fries.

SHOPPING LIST

olive oil or avocado oil

1 tablespoon cumin seeds

1 large or 2 small red onions, peeled and finely chopped

2–4 garlic cloves, peeled and finely chopped

500 g (1 lb 2 oz/3 cups) cooked black beans or 2 tins, drained

45 g (1 ½ oz /½ cup) of quick oats or 65 g (2 ¼ oz/½ cup) buckwheat flour

1 teaspoon sea salt

1 teaspoon smoked paprika

freshly ground black pepper, to taste

about 100 g (3½ oz/½ cup) corn kernels, fresh or tinned, drained

a small handful of coriander (cilantro), finely chopped

Yuca Fries (see page 96), to serve

To build the burgers:

4–6 burger buns or lettuce leaves if you are gluten-free

1 large tomato

1 large red onion

1 large avocado

a handful of coriander (cilantro)

Chipotle Mayo (see page 141)

SLOW
SUPPERS

—

FALAFEL

—

A healthy spin on my deep-fried obsession.

YOU NEED TO...

Soak the chickpeas overnight or all day in a large bowl or pot of water.

Preheat the oven to 180°C (350°F/Gas 4) and place your oven tray on the top or second to top shelf.

Drain the chickpeas and place in the food processor. Roughly chop the onion, garlic and fresh herbs and add to the food processor with all of the other ingredients except for the sesame or hemp seeds. Pulse the mixture, scraping down the sides occasionally, until the mixture resembles breadcrumbs. Be careful that you don't over-mix, or it will turn into hummus.

Once the mixture resembles breadcrumbs, use wet hands to form it into about 12 large balls, each a little bigger than a golf ball. Roll each ball in the seeds until they are evenly coated. Place on a lightly oiled baking tray.

Bake for 30 minutes, turning halfway through cooking.

NOTES

Usually I am pretty flexible with tinned vs dried legumes, depending on time restraints. But this is an exception. DO NOT USE TINNED CHICKPEAS. If you want these to turn out right, you have to do the soak.

Instead of making balls, you can use this recipe to make burger patties and either bake or pan-fry them (about 10 minutes on each side over a medium heat). I like to serve them in buns or pita pockets with fresh salad, pickles and a range of homemade dips and sauces.

SHOPPING LIST

375 g (14 oz) dried chickpeas

1 medium or ½ large white onion, peeled

5 garlic cloves, peeled

a large handful of parsley

a large handful of coriander (cilantro) (optional)

3 teaspoons cumin seeds

2 teaspoons coriander seeds

2 teaspoons sea salt

1½ teaspoons ground turmeric

1 teaspoon ground cinnamon

½ teaspoon ground cardamom

½ teaspoon cayenne pepper

lots of freshly ground black pepper

3 tablespoons olive oil

2 heaped tablespoons plain (all-purpose) or buckwheat flour

sesame or hemp seeds, for rolling

To serve:

Classic Hummus (see page 92), tahini, Baba Ganoush (see page 88), Peanut Sauce (see page 146), Tabbouleh (see page 31), fresh salad, pickles and pita

PEA AND POTATO DUMPLINGS

There is no quick way to make potato dumplings, but when you have the time, it is so worth it for these pillows of spring-flavoured heaven.

YOU NEED TO...

Preheat the oven to 180°C (350°F/Gas 4).

Scrub your potatoes, quarter, and then place in a roasting tray. Bake the potatoes for 30–40 minutes or until easily pierced with a fork.

Shell your peas and place in a large pot of boiling water. Let the peas cook for 5–10 minutes and then remove with a slotted spoon. Do not drain the water – keep it boiling for now so you can use it to test and cook your dumpling dough in later.

Mash the potatoes, peas and lemon zest until the potatoes are well broken up and the peas are all mushy. It's fine if you have some chunks. Start to mix in the flour, little by little, using a fork. When the dough starts to come together, add the remaining flour to the bowl a handful at a time and knead it using the heel of your palm.

Keep adding the flour until you have a ball of dough that is not too sticky and not too firm. Break off a small piece and test it by dropping it into the large pot of boiling water. It should float to the surface and retain its shape. If it does, you are good to go. If it falls apart, add a little more flour.

Make the rest of your dumplings. The easiest way to do this is to pull off small chunks and roll them into balls or little oval-shaped nuggets.

SHOPPING LIST

1 kg (2 lb 3 oz) large potatoes

300 g (10½ oz) snow peas

zest of 1 organic lemon (you're using zest in the dumplings so it's best to use organic if possible)

125–250 g (4–9 oz/1–2 cups) plain (all-purpose) flour (depending on the moisture in your potatoes), plus some for rolling

olive oil, for frying

sea salt and freshly ground black pepper

rocket (arugula) or another leafy green, to serve

toasted pine nuts, to garnish (optional)

Top up the large pot of water and bring it to the boil once more. Plop the dumplings into the boiling water in batches of 10–12. As they float to the surface, remove with a slotted spoon.

Place a large frying pan (skillet) on a medium heat and add a little bit of olive oil. Fry the dumplings in batches, making sure there is enough oil to prevent them from sticking to the bottom of the pan. When the undersides are golden brown, flip. If your dumplings are shaped more like balls, just jiggle them around in the pan so they cook evenly all over.

Season with salt and pepper and serve on a bed of leafy greens. Top with toasted pine nuts if you want some extra decadence.

SUPER SIMPLE DAAL

Warming and delicious, this super simple daal is the perfect after work dinner, but it if you have a little more time to spend in the kitchen and want to wow your friends with a thali, it can also be served with my Spinach and Chickpea Curry on page 44 and my Masala Mash on page 97.

YOU NEED TO...

Cook the rice according to your preferred cooking method.

Heat the coconut oil in the bottom of a medium-sized saucepan. Add the onion and cook until transparent.

Add the cumin and mustard seeds and stir until the mustard seeds pop, then add the turmeric, hing and garlic and stir for another minute. Next, add the lentils with 750 ml (25 fl oz/3 cups) of water, stir and raise the heat to high.

Chop the courgette and carrot any way you like, although my preference is thin slices. You can also grate them if you hate chopping.

Once the daal is boiling, lower the heat to a simmer and continue to stir and add more water as it thickens. It's ready when the lentils have completely broken down.

Remove from the heat, stir in a teaspoon of salt and allow to cool a little before tasting. You may need more salt depending on your flavour preferences. Garnish with the coriander just before serving.

Serve with the rice or if you feel like being a little bit fancy, make it a feast with my Spinach and Chickpea Curry and Masala Mash.

SHOPPING LIST

400 g (12 oz/2 cups) Basmati rice

1 tablespoon coconut oil

1 medium white onion, peeled and finely chopped

2 teaspoons cumin seeds

1 teaspoon black mustard seeds

1 teaspoon turmeric

¼ teaspoon hing (asafoetida)

4 cloves garlic, peeled and finely chopped

400 g (12 oz /2 cups) red lentils

1 large courgette (zucchini)

1 large carrot

1 teaspoon salt, plus more to taste

a few leaves of coriander (cilantro), to garnish

To serve (optional):
Spinach and Chickpea Curry (see page 44)
Masala Mash (see page 97)

MUSHROOM TART

Delicious hot or cold, this is great for a casual dinner with friends or a day-trip to the countryside.

YOU NEED TO...

Preheat the oven to 180°C (350°F/Gas 4).

To make the crust, place the flour, salt and oil in a bowl and mix with a fork until the ingredients are combined but the mixture is still crumbly. Add the seeds and stir just to combine.

Slowly add 4 tablespoons of water, stirring after each addition, until the mixture sticks together. How much water you require will usually vary depending on the humidity that day. Lightly knead into a ball in the bowl and then place the ball on a floured surface.

Press the ball into a circle with your fingertips. Flip and roll flat with a lightly floured rolling pin, then continue to flip and roll again, dusting the top with a little flour each time, until your crust looks big enough to fit in your pie dish or cake tin and go up the side a little. (I prefer to use a cake tin because I like the aesthetic of the edge it produces, and it is a lot easier to clean than a regular pie dish).

Gently lift the crust into your pie dish or cake tin. Press the crust into shape with your fingers. Fix any broken bits in place by overlapping slightly and pressing to combine the edges. Prick holes in the crust using a fork. Blind bake for 20 minutes while preparing the filling.

To make the filling, lightly cover the bottom of a saucepan with olive oil and place over a medium heat. Finely chop the shallots (or onions) and add to the pan with the salt. Cook until they are soft and transparent.

While the shallots are cooking, roughly chop the mushrooms into small pieces and set aside. Add the lemon juice and all of the mushrooms to the

SHOPPING LIST

For the crust:

125 g (4 oz/1 cup) plain (all-purpose) flour, plus extra for rolling

½ teaspoon sea salt

50 ml (2 fl oz/¼ cup) olive oil

4 tablespoons small seeds, such as hemp, sesame, poppy

For the filling:

olive oil

3 shallots (or 2 small white onions), peeled

1 teaspoon sea salt

800 g (1 lb 12 oz) assorted mushrooms

juice of 1 lemon

225 g (8 oz/1½ cups) cooked white beans or 250 ml (8½ fl oz/1 cup) plant-based yoghurt of your choice

3 tablespoons plain (all-purpose) flour

1 teaspoon dried lovage, if available, otherwise a sprinkling of powdered vegetable stock

1 teaspoon smoked paprika or chilli flakes

2 garlic cloves, peeled

large handful of flat-leaf (Italian) parsley

additional fresh herbs of your choice (basil, rosemary, thyme and sage all work wonderfully)

freshly ground black pepper, to taste

a handful of toasted pine nuts, to serve

leafy greens or salad, to serve

pan. Stir until the mushrooms begin to shrink and release liquid. While the mushrooms are cooking, drain and rinse the white beans, if using, and blend them into a smooth paste.

Once the mushrooms are soft and cooked, add the flour and spices in two batches, stirring to combine after each addition. Add the puréed beans or yoghurt, chopped garlic, fresh herbs and black pepper. Stir some more, making sure to scrape the spoon to remove any stuck-on floury, mushroomy, spicy goodness.

Pour the filling into the crust and top with the toasted pine nuts. Bake for 30–40 minutes. Let stand for 10 minutes before serving. Serve the tart on its own, with leafy greens or a green salad.

LASAGNE

This is a little bit messy and time-consuming, but fun to make with friends if you allocate a different part of the prep to each person and then build it, bake it, drink some wine – and eat it!

YOU NEED TO...

Prepare the tomato sauce and Cashew Cream following the recipes, adding the finely chopped garlic and nutmeg to the cream when blending.

Preheat the oven to 180°C (350°F/Gas mark 4).

Heat a chargrill pan to high. Cut the courgettes into 5 mm (¼ in) thick slices on a long diagonal. Brush the grill pan with avocado oil, place the courgette slices over it and sprinkle them with salt. Allow to cook for 4–5 minutes or until grill lines appear. Flip and cook for another 4–5 minutes and then transfer to a plate and repeat with the remaining slices.

Heat a little olive oil in the bottom of a saucepan over a medium heat. Add the chopped shallots and cook for a few minutes. Next add the mushrooms and stir until they begin to release liquid. Remove the thick stems from the chard or kale, cut the leaves in half and then into thin slices and add to the shallot and mushroom mix.

Place the peas in a saucepan of cold water and cook them on a high heat. When the water is boiled, the peas are ready – regardless of whether they were fresh or frozen.

Build the lasagne by covering the bottom of your dish with lasagne sheets. Spoon a third of the tomato sauce over the sheets. Top with the peas. Pour a third of the Cashew Cream over.

SHOPPING LIST

1 portion of Fresh Tomato Napoli Sauce (see page 138)

2 portions of Cashew Cream (see page 140) (you can get away with 1 or 1½ portions if 2 is a bit decadent)

1 garlic clove, peeled and finely chopped

½ teaspoon ground nutmeg

3 large courgettes (zucchini)

avocado oil, to brush the pan

sea salt, to taste

olive oil

1 shallot, peeled and finely chopped

200–400 g (7–14 oz) brown mushrooms, finely sliced

a large bunch of chard or kale

235 g (8 oz/1½ cups) peas, freshly shelled or frozen

enough lasagne sheets to make 3 layers in whatever dish you are using

a small handful of hemp seeds or pine nuts (or both)

basil leaves, to garnish

Place another layer of lasagne sheets over the pea layer, another third of the tomato sauce, the shallot, mushroom and chard mix and then another third of the Cashew Cream.

Finish with a layer of lasagne sheets and the remainder of the tomato sauce. Arrange the courgette slices nicely over the top and drizzle over the remaining Cashew Cream. Top with a sprinkling of hemp seeds or pine nuts.

Cook the lasagne, covered, in the oven for 45 minutes and uncovered for a further 15 minutes. Allow to sit for 10 minutes before serving. Top with few leaves of fresh basil, to garnish.

NOTES

You can buy ready-made tomato sauce if you don't have time to make your own. You can also make the sauce more 'meaty' by adding lentils as in the Bolognese recipe on page 36. For a super simple lasagne, skip the veggies and just use lasagne sheets, tomato sauce and Cashew Cream.

Pumpkin (squash) and aubergine (eggplant) also work great in place of courgette (zucchini), as do asparagus spears. Be experimental. This recipe is incredibly versatile and always delicious.

NUT ROAST

—

The plant-based alternative to meatloaf or a roast, this is always the first thing to go at family dinners because it is so damn delicious – and you don't have to be vegan or vegetarian to appreciate it!

YOU NEED TO...

Preheat the oven to 190°C (375°F/Gas 5).

Place the cashew nuts, almonds, sunflower seeds, walnuts, sesame seeds, linseeds, poppy seeds, powdered veggie stock, psyllium husk (or chia seeds) and olive oil in a food processor with 100 ml (3½ fl oz/ ⅓ cup) of water and blend until the nuts are well chopped. Add to a large mixing bowl with the remaining ingredients and season to taste. Stir well.

Line a 28 cm (11 in) loaf tin with parchment, spoon the mixture into the tin and press flat with the back of a spoon. You want it to be quite firm. Sprinkle sesame seeds on top and bake for 1 hour, turning halfway to ensure even baking – especially if your oven is a dodgy old codger like mine.

Allow to cool for 10 minutes before serving. Serve with Mushroom Gravy, roasted veggies and a big yummy salad.

NOTES

Psyllium husk will give you a firm loaf, whilst chia seeds will give you a more crumbly loaf. Both are delicious.

CH-CH-CH-CH-CHANGES...

Be creative! This is my 'ideal' nut roast, but if you want to use other nuts and seeds you have on hand, do so! Just keep the ratios about the same.

SHOPPING LIST

155 g (5½ oz/1 cup) cashew nuts

155 g (5½ oz/½ cup) almonds

125 g (4 oz/1 cup) sunflower seeds

125 g (4 oz/½ cup) walnuts

2 tablespoons each of sesame, linseed and poppy seeds, plus extra sesame seeds to sprinkle on top

1 teaspoon powdered veggie stock

4 tablespoons psyllium husk or chia seeds

100 ml (3½ fl oz/⅓ cup) olive oil

juice of 1 lemon

1 medium onion, peeled and finely chopped

3 garlic cloves, peeled and finely chopped

6 mushrooms, finely chopped

1 large courgette (zucchini), grated

3 tablespoons flour (plain, rice or buckwheat)

1 tablespoon finely chopped winter savory or flat-leaf (Italian) parsley

1 tablespoon other dried herbs, such as thyme or rosemary

½ teaspoon chilli flakes or smoked paprika (optional)

sea salt and freshly ground black pepper

To serve:

Mushroom Gravy (see page 139)

roasted veggies of your choice

leafy salad

VEGAN GOODNESS

PIZZA! PIZZA! PIZZA!

——

Proof that pizza is awesome without cheese!

YOU NEED TO...

Place the flour, salt and yeast in a large bowl and use a fork to combine. Add the olive oil and water, a little at a time, to the bowl and stir everything together until it forms a loose ball.

Sprinkle some flour on a large, clean surface. Dump the dough mixture onto the flour and knead for a couple of minutes, until you have one nice big smooth ball. If it's not behaving, let it rest a minute or two while you wash and dry the bowl and then come back to it.

Place a little bit of olive oil in the bottom of the bowl, plop the ball in there, cover with a clean tea towel (dish towel) and leave it somewhere warmish until it has doubled in size. This usually takes an hour but it can take up to 2, depending on where you live. Use this time to prep any ingredients and toppings and don't clean up the flour mess unless you really need to, as you will need it again later.

Once the dough has doubled, punch it to get the air out and then dump it back out onto the floured counter. Divide into the number of pizzas you wish to make and then form each of these pieces into an approximate ball shape. Cover with the tea towel and allow to sit for about 20 minutes.

Preheat the oven to 220°C (425°F/Gas 7).

On the same floury surface, roll your dough out, base by base. I like to press the ball flat, sprinkle a little flour on top, roll over it a couple of times with a rolling pin, flip it over, roll some more in the opposite direction, then swiftly but gently transfer to a tray.

SHOPPING LIST

375 g (13 oz/3 cups) plain (all-purpose) flour, plus extra for rolling

2 teaspoons sea salt

2 teaspoons or 1 packet dried yeast

2 tablespoons olive oil, plus extra for the bowl

250 ml (8½ fl oz/1 cup) lukewarm water

For the toppings:
see opposite page

Saving any greens for when the pizza is out of the oven, add the toppings of your choice (see below) and bake the pizza for 10–12 minutes or until the crust is crisp and golden but not burnt (unless burnt is your jam, in which case go ahead and leave it for a little longer until it gets all burnt and blistery). Remove the pizza from the oven, add any salady greens and additional sauces – and eat!

ABOUT THE TOPPINGS

This is where you can really let loose, either using up what's in the fridge or creating toppings especially for your pizzas. I like to keep it quite minimal, hence I prefer to make lots of small pizzas rather than one big one. Some favourite combos are (as pictured overleaf):

— Potato, rosemary and sea salt. This really is the best pizza in the whole damn land. Brush the dough with some olive oil, cover with thin slices of boiled potato, sprinkle with rosemary and sea salt and go to heaven.
— Green Pesto (see page 136), Caramelised Onions (see page 149), cherry tomatoes and pine nuts.
— Caramelised Onions (see page 149), fig and walnut with rocket (arugula) and balsamic vinegar.
— Tomato, pumpkin (squash) and olives with Cashew Cream (see page 140) and microgreens.
— Sun-dried tomatoes, artichoke hearts, roasted red (bell) peppers, roasted aubergine (eggplant), roasted courgette (zucchini) and vegan cream cheese also make great toppings.

Clockwise from the top: Green pesto, caramelised onions, cherry tomatoes and pine nuts; Caramelised onions, fig and walnut with rocket and balsamic vinegar; Potato, rosemary and sea salt; Tomato, pumpkin and olives with cashew cream and micro greens

ROLLATINI

This dish is a commitment. It's messy and it takes time, but it is so so so worth it. You can prepare some or all of the ingredients the day before if you like.

YOU NEED TO...

Slice the top off each aubergine and then cut lengthways into long strips, so that you have 16 slices. Lay the slices flat on clean tea towels (dish towels). Sprinkle with salt and allow to sit for a couple of hours.

Preheat the oven to 180°C (350°F/Gas 4).

Brush a baking tray with a little olive oil, place the aubergine on the tray and brush a tiny bit of oil on the top. Bake for 20 minutes, then allow to cool while you prepare everything else.

Prepare the tomato sauce and Cashew Cream as per the recipes. Pour a teeny-tiny drizzle of olive oil into a frying pan (skillet) and place over a medium–low heat. Finely chop the mushrooms, walnuts and spinach and add to the pan. Once the pan is filled with liquid, increase the heat to medium–high and stir frequently until all the liquid has evaporated.

Stir three-quarters of the Cashew Cream into the mushroom and spinach mixture and stir. Season well with black pepper.

Place a tablespoon of the filling onto each aubergine slice, top with a basil leaf and roll it up, then place it in a lasagne dish with the 'seam' on the bottom. Repeat with each piece. Spoon the tomato sauce over everything and place in the oven for half an hour. Drizzle with the remaining Cashew Cream before serving with some crusty bread or green salad.

SHOPPING LIST

3–4 large aubergines (eggplants)
sea salt
olive oil
1 portion of Fresh Tomato Napoli Sauce (see page 138)
1 portion of Cashew Cream (see page 140)
20 medium brown mushrooms
150 g (5 oz/1½ cups) walnuts
200 g (7 oz/4 cups) baby spinach
16 fresh basil leaves
freshly ground black pepper

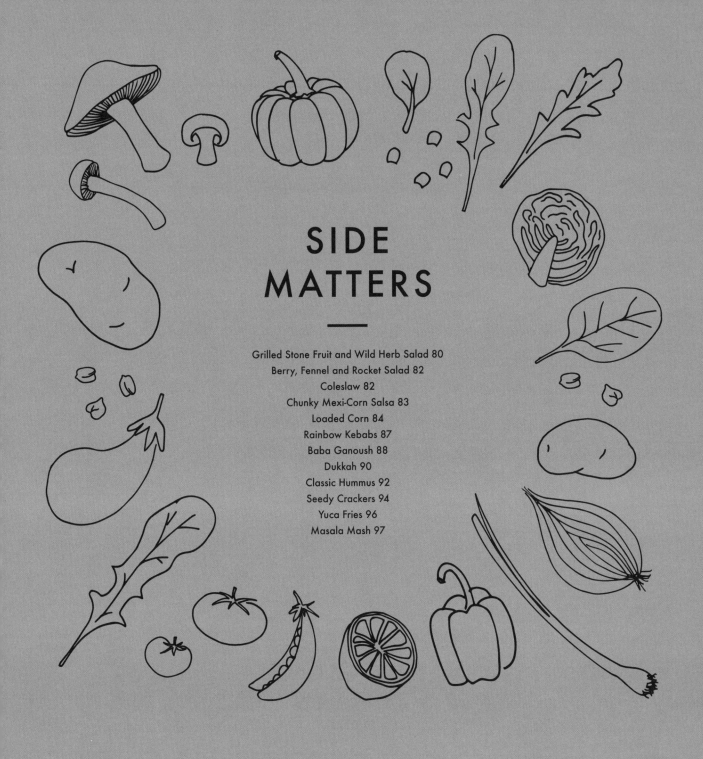

SIDE
MATTERS

—

GRILLED STONE FRUIT AND WILD HERB SALAD

——

A combination of tangy, slightly caramelised stone fruits with wild herbs and a simple balsamic dressing.

YOU NEED TO...

Light a barbecue or put a chargrill pan on the stovetop over a high heat. Cut each piece of fruit in half or quarters and remove the stone.

Brush the barbecue or chargrill pan with oil and place the fruit on it, skin side down, remembering which piece you placed down first so it can be your 'tester'.

Leave the fruit on the heat for about 5 minutes and then check. If nice black lines have appeared, turn the fruit over so that the fleshy side is now touching the barbecue. After another 5 minutes, remove.

Arrange the wild herbs on a board, top with fruit and drizzle with the balsamic glaze. Season.

NOTES

Choose fruit that is still quite firm so that it doesn't disintegrate on the grill. If you want, you can grill the fruit ahead of time and use the following day when it is cold.

SHOPPING LIST

2–4 each of nectarines, peaches and apricots

an oil with a high smoke point such as avocado oil

3 large handfuls of wild herbs or rocket (arugula)

balsamic glaze (crema di balsamico)

sea salt and freshly ground black pepper

BERRY, FENNEL AND ROCKET SALAD

——

A perfect summer side salad.

YOU NEED TO...

Place the rocket in a bowl or on a plate or chopping board. Finely slice the fennel (using a mandoline if you have one), and place this on top of the rocket.

Place the berries on top of the fennel. Drizzle with the balsamic glaze and season with freshly ground black pepper.

SHOPPING LIST

3 handfuls of rocket (arugula)

1 fennel bulb

3 handfuls of berries (sliced if using strawberries)

balsamic glaze (crema di balsamico) or vinegar

freshly ground black pepper

SERVES 4–6 AS A SIDE OR IN BURGERS, WRAPS, TACOS, BAKED POTATOES

COLESLAW

——

Who says vegans can't enjoy creamy, delicious coleslaw? This is quick to make and is so yummy it has even fooled the most carnivorous of family members who think that vegans only eat iceberg lettuce.

YOU NEED TO...

Finely chop the cabbage, then peel and julienne or grate the carrot. If using an apple, peel and grate this too. Combine in a bowl with the dressing and seeds. Stir in the parsley, if using, and season to taste.

SHOPPING LIST

¼ red, green or savoy cabbage

3 large carrots, peeled

1 Granny Smith apple (optional but totally delicious)

1 portion of Creamy Tahini Dressing (see page 145) or 60 g (2 oz/¼ cup) vegan mayo (but you know which one I think tastes better)

a large handful of toasted pumpkin, sunflower or sesame seeds or all three

a small handful of flat-leaf (Italian) parsley (optional), finely chopped

sea salt and freshly ground black pepper

CHUNKY MEXI-CORN SALSA

——

So simple, yet so delicious.

YOU NEED TO...

If you are using tinned corn, place it in a sieve and allow it to drain while you prep the remaining ingredients. If using fresh corn, bring a pot of water to the boil, remove the husks from the corn and cut each cob in half. Once the water is boiling, place the corn in the pot and cook for approximately 3 minutes, then remove. Allow to cool as you prep your remaining ingredients.

Finely chop the red onion and place in a medium-sized bowl. Dice the tomatoes and pepper and add to the bowl, making sure you scoop up all the juices and seeds from the tomato. Chop the coriander and add along with the sweetcorn. If you're using corn on the cob, remove the kernels with a knife. Juice the lime and add this to the bowl with a little salt. Use a spoon or your hands to combine everything.

Serve with corn chips and guacamole or with my Jackfruit Tacos (see page 40) or Quick Nachos (see page 25).

NOTES

Use the ingredients as a guide only. A big red onion is OK instead of a small one, and you can use more tomatoes or corn than I have suggested. I wouldn't recommend using a white onion in place of the red onion, but spring onions (scallions) are totally fine. If you hate coriander (cilantro), skip it and try parsley or basil instead. Add chilli if you like.

SHOPPING LIST

1 x 220 g (8 oz) jar or tin of sweetcorn (corn kernels) or 2 cobs of corn

1 small red onion, peeled

2–3 tomatoes

1 medium red (bell) pepper

a large handful of coriander (cilantro) leaves

1 lime

sea salt flakes, to garnish

TURN IT INTO A MEAL

Add a tin of black beans, some baby spinach or rocket (arugula) and some chopped avocado. Serves 2 or 3.

LOADED CORN

—

Whether it is the star of the show or a side dish, loaded corn is always a crowd favourite.

YOU NEED TO...

Make your Cashew Cream and finely chop the coriander, spring onions and chilli (if using fresh). I do this at home and then pop it in a container to take to the park where we barbecue. However, if you are cooking the corn at home, then you can prep everything while the corn is cooking.

Heat a barbecue or chargrill pan. Peel the corn, leaving the husks on but removing all the stringy bits. Brush the corn with the avocado oil and place on the barbecue or pan. When the corn starts to blacken on the underside (about 5 minutes), turn it so that the next quarter starts to cook. Continue to do this until it is cooked all over.

Place all of the cooked corn on a serving plate. Drizzle with Cashew Cream, top with the chopped coriander, spring onions, chilli and salt. Squeeze lime over the top. Eat!

NOTES

Avocado oil has the highest smoke point of all of the oils, which is why I use it for grilling. If you don't have access to it, the next best thing is coconut oil (really yummy on corn) or extra light olive oil. If you are not up-to-date with smoke points and oils, in a nutshell: when an oil is heated over its smoke point it breaks down, rendering it not only ineffective as a non-stick agent, but also harmful to your health.

Vegan mayo works really well instead of Cashew Cream, as does Chipotle Mayo (see page 141).

SHOPPING LIST

Cashew Cream (see page 140)
a bunch of coriander (cilantro)
2–4 spring onions (scallions)
fresh or dried chilli, to taste
8 cobs of corn
avocado oil
sea salt flakes
1–4 limes, cut into quaters

RAINBOW KEBABS

—

You can use any veggies you like, including potato or sweet potato if you boil it first, but if you wanna make a rainbow, I suggest the ingredients below. If using wooden skewers, soak these in water before threading on the veggies to prevent them catching fire on the barbecue.

YOU NEED TO...

Combine the marinade ingredients in a large bowl. Add the vegetables and toss so that they are evenly coated in marinade. Leave for half an hour or overnight.

Preheat the barbecue or chargrill pan.

Thread the veggies onto 8 skewers. Place on the barbecue or pan for 5 minutes or until the underside is blackened, then turn and cook the other side for another 5 minutes or until it begins to go black.

Serve alone or on a bed of greens or grains, plain or drizzled with balsamic glaze and pomegranate seeds, with hummus or pesto or both.

SHOPPING LIST

For the marinade:

30 ml (1 fl oz) avocado oil

30 ml (1 fl oz) balsamic vinegar

½ teaspoon harissa paste

sea salt and freshly gorund black pepper

For the kebabs:

8 cherry tomatoes

1–2 orange (bell) peppers, cut into 2.5 cm (1 in) squares

8 apricots or other stoned fruits, halved and the stone removed

1 or 2 large courgettes (zucchini), cut into 2.5 cm (1 in) pieces

1 large red onion, peeled and cut into quarters and then each quarter in half

8 small brown mushrooms

8 small radishes

To serve (optional):

leafy greens or grains, balsamic glaze, pomegranate seeds, Classic Hummus (see page 92), Green Pesto (see page 136)

BABA GANOUSH

———

The unique, smoky taste of baba ganoush comes from the process of blackening the aubergine. I like to blitz mine so it's smooth, but you can also use a fork if you prefer something a little more rustic and chunky. Either way, it's delicious.

YOU NEED TO...

First, blacken the aubergine. Preheat your oven to its highest temperature. Pierce the aubergine a few times with a fork, place it on a baking tray on the top shelf (or second-to-top if your aubergine is too big) and cook for around 5–10 minutes, until the skin is black and blistering. Turn over and repeat. Alternatively – if you are lucky enough to have a gas stove or barbecue – you can place it over an open flame and turn with tongs as it blackens and blisters.

While the aubergine is cooling, prepare the other ingredients. There's not much to do here really, just roughly chop the garlic and juice the lemon.

Once the aubergine is cool, cut it open and scoop out the flesh. Some people like to discard the seeds, but I keep mine because it seems a shame to throw them away. Place the flesh in a bowl or blending receptacle with the chopped garlic, lemon juice, tahini, olive oil, cumin seeds, paprika and some salt. Being the salty lady that I am, I like to use about 1 teaspoon of salt flakes. If you're less salty, start with ½ teaspoon. Mash with a fork or blend with a food procrespor, until everything is thoroughly combined.

Put the dip into a new serving bowl and garnish with the parsley and toasted pine nuts or flaked almonds. If not eating immediately, chill until ready to eat.

Serve with Seedy Crackers, salty corn chips, Falafel, soft bread or toasted bread. Anything that calls for a dip, really.

SHOPPING LIST

1 large or 2 medium-sized aubergines (eggplants)
2 garlic cloves (optional), peeled
½ lemon
1 generous tablespoon tahini
a drizzle of olive oil
1 teaspoon cumin seeds
½ teaspoon smoked paprika (optional)
sea salt flakes
a handful of flat-leaf (Italian) parsley, finely chopped, to garnish
toasted pine nuts or flaked almonds, to garnish

To serve:
Seedy Crakers (see page 94), salty corn chips, Falafel (see page 58) or bread

DUKKAH

—

Dukkah is traditionally served with fresh bread and a high-quality olive oil. You dunk the bread into the oil, then into the dukkah, then pop it in your mouth. It's delicious! We use dukkah on all kinds of things, on top of any kind of roasted or mashed vegetable, salad, avocado on toast, white bean mash, you name it – sometimes we even eat it straight from the jar.

Preheat the oven to 180°C (350°F/Gas 4).

Spread the nuts on a baking tray and toast for 10 minutes or until lightly brown and fragrant. Remove and allow to cool on the baking tray (they will continue to cook a little on here so if you accidentally let them go too brown, remove them from the tray).

While the nuts are cooling, place a non-stick pan on a medium–high heat and toast the sesame, cumin and coriander seeds for 2–3 minutes until fragrant and you hear them crackle ever so quietly. Remove from the heat and transfer to a dinner plate or something similar so they don't continue to cook.

When the nuts are cool, place in a food processor and blend until lightly chopped. Add the seeds, salt and paprika and blend some more until the nuts are well chopped and everything is combined and almost powdery. Grind the pepper into the mix and pulse once to combine.

Serve immediately or store in a clean, airtight jar until ready to use.

175 g (6 oz/1 cup) nuts of your choice (I use almonds and hazelnuts. If using hazelnuts, either buy them without skins or remove the skins using the method below)

30 g (1 oz/¼ cup) sesame seeds

1 tablespoon cumin seeds

1 tablespoon coriander seeds

⅓ teaspoon sea salt

½ teaspoon smoked paprika or chilli flakes (optional)

¼ teaspoon freshly ground black pepper

NOTES

You can use nuts that are already toasted and salted, but reduce the amount of salt you then add to the mix. You can also use ground spices, however, they will only need 1 minute in the pan with the sesame seeds.

TO REMOVE THE SKINS FROM HAZELNUTS

Place the still-warm toasted hazelnuts on a damp tea towel (dish towel). Wrap up like a Christmas cracker and roll back and forth like a rolling pin to make the skins come off OR use a scrubbing brush over the top of the tea towel to loosen up the skins. They won't all come off, but this is OK (however, it's best to remove some, or your dukkah might be bitter).

CLASSIC HUMMUS

The delicious and nutritious vegan staple with infinite variations.

YOU NEED TO...

Blend the ingredients together with a splash of water until well combined. Continue to blend, adding water a little at a time, to the desired consistency (more water will make your hummus creamier). Season to taste.

Enjoy immediately or store in a clean, airtight container in the fridge for up to 5 days. I find it tastes best the next day, so if I am making it for a picnic or dinner party I always try to make it the day before.

ALTERNATIVE FLAVOURS

Try adding some of the following if you need a change from your usual hummus flavour or if you have some spare veggies that need using up:
— Beetroot (beets) – red or yellow, roasted or boiled
— Pumpkin (squash) – roasted or boiled
— Any kind of leafy green – spinach, kale, coriander (cilantro), parsley,
— Olives – 10–20 pitted black olives
— Sweet potato – roasted or boiled
— Sweet (bell) peppers – any colour, slow-roasted or pickled taste best
— Superfood powders – turmeric, spirulina (combine with a little water first)
— Semi-dried tomatoes or sun-dried tomatoes
— Make your hummus with white beans instead of chickpeas.
The world is your chickpea my friend...

IT'S DELICIOUS ON...

I don't even know how to begin listing the ways in which you can enjoy this. For starters, with crackers, in a sandwich, with mashed or baked potatoes, in any burger, with my Falafels (see page 58)...

SHOPPING LIST

250 g (9 oz/1½ cups) cooked or tinned chickpeas
2 garlic cloves, peeled
1–2 tablespoons tahini
juice of ½ lemon
a splash of olive oil
1 teaspoon ground cumin
½ teaspoon sea salt

Clockwise from the top: Leafy green; Olives; Beetroot; Classic; Pumpkin

VEGAN GOODNESS

SEEDY CRACKERS

———

This is a recipe that floated into my mind while falling asleep one night. I tried it the next day, expecting to tweak it at least a little, but it turned out perfectly and has been a household staple ever since.

YOU NEED TO...

Preheat the oven to 180°C (350°F/Gas 4).

Place all the ingredients in a food processor with 5 tablespoons of water and pulse a few times. Scrape down the sides and continue to pulse and scrape until everything is finely chopped and the mixture feels sticky. Dump the mixture out onto a sheet of baking parchment. Form it into a ball and then flatten it out a little with your hands.

Place another sheet of baking parchment over the mix and gently start to roll it out with a rolling pin or wine bottle. I like to do this on a table and hold the edges of the baking parchment in place by leaning against it so that it doesn't slip all over the place. Go up and down and left and right so that you have a large flat continent of cracker mix taking up about two-thirds of the baking parchment. The edges will crumble a little but this is fine – I like the character it adds to the crackers.

Remove the top layer of baking parchment and use a large sharp kitchen knife or pizza cutter to cut the crackers to the desired size, using a pressing down motion as opposed to a slicing motion. I generally make mine in 4 cm (1½ in) squares. Sprinkle some additional sea salt or seeds on top now if you like (big chunks of flaky salt taste reeeally good).

Lift the piece of baking parchment onto a baking tray and place in the oven for 20–25 minutes. You may have to rotate the tray once during cooking to prevent the crackers at the back from burning.

Remove from the oven and allow to cool on the tray, then gently peel them off the baking parchment and place in an airtight container until ready to eat.

SHOPPING LIST

30 g (1 oz/¼ cup) linseeds or flaxseeds, plus extra to sprinkle

40 g (1½ oz/¼ cup) sesame seeds, plus extra to sprinkle

30 g (1 oz/¼ cup) sunflower seeds, plus extra to sprinkle

40 g (1½ oz/¼ cup) poppy seeds, plus extra to sprinkle

1 tablespoon olive oil

½ teaspoon sea salt, plus extra to sprinkle

1 teaspoon cumin seeds

CH-CH-CH-CH-CHANGES...

The great thing about this recipe is that you can use any seeds you have on hand. Hemp seeds and pumpkin seeds work wonderfully, as do almond flakes. Just don't skimp on the linseeds, as they are the glue in this mix. Without them, your crackers won't hold their form, unless you are replacing them with chia seeds or psyllium husk.

— Add coriander seeds instead of cumin seeds.
— Add chipotle or chilli flakes if you like a spicy cracker.
— Omit the cumin and 1 tablespoon of water and use algae flakes and tamari for an Asian twist.
— Avocado, sesame, walnut and coconut oils are all delicious alternatives to olive.

A NOTE ABOUT LINSEEDS

Buy whole, not ground, linseeds, as ground can go rancid and ruin the taste of an entire dish.

YUCA FRIES

If you are one of those people who loves fishing around in a pile of fries for all the little crispy bits, then you will loooove Yuca Fries. After you boil them, they start to break apart a little, giving them maximum surface area for that crispy goodness. This is the perfect accompaniment for the Black Bean Burgers (see page 54).

YOU NEED TO...

Preheat the oven to 180°C (350°F/Gas 4).

Cut the yuca through the middle and then place the open end flat on the chopping board and carefully cut the tough skin away in downward strokes (hold it at the top so as to protect your fingers).

Once the skin is removed, cut the yuca into thick fries and then place in a large saucepan of water with the sugar and 1 teaspoon of the salt. Bring to the boil and allow to simmer for 10 minutes until they are just starting to become pierceable with a fork.

Drain the water and add the avocado oil and remaining salt to the pan. Place the lid on top and shake until all of the fries are well coated.

Spread the fries in a single layer on one or two baking trays and place in the oven for 10–15 minutes. Remove, flip and cook for another 10–15 minutes or until golden brown.

Sprinkle with dried parsley and serve.

NOTES

This method also works great for straight-up potato fries.

SHOPPING LIST

2 large yuca (cassava), peeled

4 tablespoons granulated (raw) brown sugar (demerara)

2 teaspoons sea salt

avocado or olive oil

2 tablespoons dried parsley

MASALA MASH

—

This way of making potatoes is so yummy that I often serve them as a stand-alone dish. If you love potatoes, they are also a really delicious rice alternative for Indian curries.

YOU NEED TO...

Scrub the potatoes, but leave the skins on, then cut into 2.5 cm (1 in) pieces. Put the potatoes in a large saucepan filled with water and place over a high heat. Bring to the boil and then lower to a medium heat and cook until easily pierced with a fork – about 20 minutes.

Drain the potatoes in a colander, rinse and dry the pan and return it to the heat.

Melt the coconut oil in the pan, then add the spices and stir for 2 minutes or until fragrant. Remove from the heat and return the potatoes to the pan with a splash of milk, then mash. Add some more milk a little at a time, until the desired consistency is reached.

Stir in salt and pepper to taste, spoon onto plates and top with a delicious hot curry.

NOTES

If you want a plain mash, just omit the spices!

SHOPPING LIST

500 g (1 lb 2 oz) large potatoes

2 tablespoons coconut oil

1 teaspoon cumin seeds

1 teaspoon coriander seeds

a pinch of hing (asafoetida)

nut milk of some kind (coconut, almond, rice and cashew are all pretty good)

sea salt and freshly ground black pepper

SWEET
TREATS

—

HOLY SHIT CAKE

——

This is a recipe from my mum that I have veganised. I renamed it Holy Shit Cake because that is what people say when they first bite into it. If you don't have a food processor you can use pre-ground nuts. The texture will be a little different, but still really yummy.

YOU NEED TO...

Preheat the oven to 180°C (350°F/Gas 4).

To make the caramel, put the coconut milk in a small saucepan. Add the chopped dates to the pan and bring to the boil, then allow to simmer, whisking occasionally to help the dates break down. When the caramel is thick and smooth, remove from the heat, add the salt and set aside.

To make the cake, blend the flaxseeds or chia seeds with 120 ml (4 fl oz/½ cup) of water and set aside. Combine the remaining ingredients, except the coconut oil, in a food processor. Pulse until the nuts are roughly chopped. Now add the flaxseeds or chia seeds and the coconut oil and blitz until thoroughly combined.

Press two-thirds of the mixture into a lined springform cake tin. Smooth the surface using the back of a wet spoon. Pour the salted caramel into the cake pan over the cake mix, using a rubber spatula so you don't miss any salted caramel goodness. Sprinkle the remaining cake mix over the caramel. Top with a handful of roughly chopped nuts.

Bake for 30 minutes and allow to cool in the tin for another 30 minutes before serving with some coconut cream or Banana Ice Cream.

CH-CH-CH-CH-CHANGES!

You can use psyllium husk instead of flax or chia seeds, but add it with the dry ingredients and then add the water with the coconut oil. Don't combine the psyllium husk with water and allow it to thicken as it will go reeeeally thick if you do this. If you are gluten-free, use gluten-free oats or rice flakes.

SHOPPING LIST

For the salted caramel:
400 ml (13 fl oz) tin coconut milk
10 Medjool dates, pits removed and finely chopped
a pinch of sea salt

For the cake:
2 tablespoons ground flaxseeds or chia seeds
140 g (5 oz/1 cup) almonds, hazelnuts or walnuts or a mix of all three, plus a handful extra, roughly chopped, for the top
40 g (1½ oz/¼ cup) sesame seeds (optional)
150 g (5 oz/1½ cups) rolled (porridge) oats or rice flakes
90 g (3¼ oz/1 cup) desiccated coconut
110 g (3¾ oz/½ cup) granulated (raw) brown sugar (demerara)
3 tablespoons plain (all-purpose) flour or buckwheat flour
1 teaspoon baking powder
1 teaspoon bicarbonate of soda (baking soda)
2 teaspoons ground cinnamon
1 teaspoon vanilla powder or extract
a pinch of sea salt
100 ml (3½ fl oz/⅓ cup) coconut oil, melted

To serve:
coconut cream or Banana Ice Cream (see page 116)

CHOCOLATE CHIP COOKIES

——

My mum taught me that cookies are always ready when you can smell them, as they will continue to cook on the tray after you remove them from the oven. I like to push it a little with these, leaving them in for a few minutes after their aroma first hits my nose. Crispy on the outside, chewy on the inside, these are a definite crowd pleaser.

YOU NEED TO...

Preheat the oven to 180°C (350°F/Gas 4) and put a piece of baking parchment on a baking tray.

Put the wet ingredients in a small bowl and stir to combine. Combine the dry ingredients, except the nuts and chocolate, in a large bowl.

Pour the wet mix into the dry mix and stir with a comfortable tablespoon to combine. Add the nuts and chocolate and stir some more until just combined.

Spoon tablespoon-sized dollops onto the baking tray, spacing them out as much as possible. Don't flatten. They will spread a little, but you should be able to get 10–20 on a tray without them becoming one giant cookie.

Bake for 25 minutes or until slightly golden on the top. Allow to cool on the tray for a few minutes before moving to a wire rack to cool completely.

CH-CH-CH-CH-CHANGES...

You can also make about 20 little cookies if you like. Just keep an eye (nose) on them to make sure they don't burn – 20 minutes should be about right here. And if you wanna be really naughty, sandwich them together with nut butter or Banana Ice Cream (see page 116). HEAVEN.

SHOPPING LIST

The wet ingredients:
175 g (6 oz/¾ cup) granulated (raw) brown sugar (demerara)
125 ml (4 fl oz/½ cup) coconut oil, melted
125 ml (4 fl oz/½ cup) nut milk

The dry ingredients:
275 g (10 oz/2¼ cups) plain (all-purpose) flour
2 teaspoons baking powder
½ teaspoon sea salt
1 teaspoon ground cinnamon
½ teaspoon cayenne pepper (optional)
1 teaspoon bourbon vanilla powder
a large handful of hazelnuts, almonds, peanuts or raisins
200 g (7 oz/1½ cups) vegan chocolate chips or vegan chocolate, roughly chopped

BUCKWHEAT PIKELETS

In New Zealand, we call little pancakes, 'pikelets'!

YOU NEED TO...

Place a frying pan over a medium heat.

Place all the dry ingredients in a bowl and then whisk in the milk. The mixture will thicken after a couple of minutes. This is the psyllium husk working its magic. If it gets too thick, add a little more milk or water and whisk it in.

Melt a little coconut oil in the bottom of the pan and dollop tablespoon-sized blobs of pancake mix into the pan. I like to do 3 at a time so that I still have space to flip them. When little bubbles start to appear and then pop, loosen the bottom of the pancakes from the pan using your spatula and then flip.

Allow to cook on the other side for about 2–3 minutes until golden. You can see when they are cooked as they stop rising and the edges no longer look wet.

Remove the pancakes from the pan using the metal spatula and place on a plate. Repeat until you have used up all of the mixture. Serve on a plate with toppings of your choice.

NOTES

These are quite absorbent little dudes so you will go through a decent amount of coconut oil. Don't be alarmed though, coconut oil is good for you!

SHOPPING LIST

130 g (4½ oz/1 cup) buckwheat flour
1 tablespoon psyllium husk
2 tablespoons granulated (raw) brown sugar (demerara)
1 teaspoon baking powder
a pinch of sea salt
1–2 teaspoons ground cinnamon
250 ml (8½ fl oz/1 cup) nut milk of your choice
coconut oil, for frying

For the toppings (optional):
maple or date syrup, banana, berries, poached fruit, coconut, nuts

Clockwise from top left: Black Bean Brownie; Pear and Caramel Tart; Tangy Berry Tarts; Matcha Cheesecake; Holy Shit Cake; Banana Bread; Chocolate Chip Cookies; Lemon and Poppy Seed Cake; Straight-Up Chocolate Cake

MATCHA CHEESECAKE

———

**In the words of my best friend, this is vegan food porn at its finest!
If you've been storing your dates in the fridge they may be a little dry.
Adding a teaspoon of water will help.**

YOU NEED TO...

Soak the cashew nuts in water for at least 4 hours and then drain,
or boil for 15 minutes.

Preheat the oven to 180°C (350°F/Gas 4).

To make the base, place the coconut and sesame seeds on a baking
tray and toast for 10 minutes, tossing once after 5 minutes.

Place the dates, toasted sesame seeds and coconut and salt in a food
processor and blend until the dates are finely chopped and you can press the
mixture together with your fingertips. Press into the bottom of your cake tin.

For the filling, clean the food processor and then place all the
ingredients for the filling into it, not forgetting the cashew nuts, and blitz
until smooth. Taste. Add more maple syrup if you prefer it to be sweeter.

Pour the filling into the tin on top of the base, and then place it in
the freezer. Allow to set for a few hours or overnight. If setting overnight,
remove from the freezer 30 minutes before serving.

Decorate with the toppings of your choice and cut with a hot knife,
cleaning the knife between slices.

After defrosting, the cheesecake will hold its flavour and form in the
fridge for up to 4–5 days.

CH-CH-CH-CH-CHANGES...

You can make individual cakes with this if you like. Press them into muffin tin
moulds lined with cling film (plastic wrap), à la my Tangy Berry Tarts recipe
on page 123.

SHOPPING LIST

225 g (8 oz/1½ cups) cashew nuts

For the base:
60 g (2 oz/⅔ cup) desiccated coconut
100 g (3½ oz/⅔ cup) sesame seeds
10 Medjool dates, stones removed
¼ teaspoon sea salt

For the filling:
200 ml (7 fl oz/¾ cup) coconut milk
4 tablespoons maple syrup
2 teaspoons vanilla powder or extract
½ teaspoon sea salt
1 tablespoon matcha powder
a handful of mint leaves, roughly
chopped (optional)

To decorate: (optional)
edible flower petals of your choice, peanut
butter, chocolate drizzle, pistachios

PEANUT BUTTER AND CHOCOLATE GRANOLA

In Croatia, an innocent bowl of granola with chocolate hidden in it led to a full-blown obsession with chocolate breakfast cereals. This is my attempt at a healthy version.

YOU NEED TO...

Preheat the oven to 180°C (350°F/Gas 4).

Melt the coconut oil, peanut butter and maple syrup together in a medium-sized saucepan. Add the oats, nuts, sesame seeds and cacao nibs to the pan and stir until evenly coated.

Spread the oat mix on a baking tray and bake for 15 minutes.

During this time, remove the pits from the dates and finely chop into tiny pieces. It's best if you keep a wet cloth nearby so you can wipe your sticky fingers and sticky knife occasionally.

Add the dates and coconut to the oat mix, stir, and bake for another 5 minutes, keeping an eye on it as the coconut can burn very quickly. Allow to cool on the tray and then store in an airtight container. It will keep at room temperature for 1–2 weeks.

When ready to eat, serve with a nut milk of your choice and whatever fresh fruit you have available.

SHOPPING LIST

4 tablespoons coconut oil

4 tablespoons smooth or crunchy peanut butter

4 tablespoons maple syrup

200 g (7 oz/2 cups) rolled oats

150 g (5 oz/1 cup) roughly chopped nuts of your choice (hazelnuts pecans, almonds and walnuts are all good options)

80 g (3 oz/½ cup) sesame seeds

60 g (2 oz/½ cup) cacao nibs

10 Medjool dates

30 g (1 oz/½ cup) coconut flakes

To serve:

nut milk and fresh fruit of your choice

STRAIGHT-UP CHOCOLATE CAKE

—

This is an adaptation of Isa Chandra's Just Chocolate Cake from her *Post Punk Kitchen* blog (theppk.com). Because sometimes you just wanna eat a cake with all the sugar and all the gluten.

YOU NEED TO...

Preheat the oven to 180°C (350°F/Gas 4).

Whisk together the coconut milk and cider vinegar in a large bowl and leave to curdle for a moment while you line your cake tin with baking parchment.

Add the sugar, coconut oil, vanilla and almond extract to the milk mix and whisk to combine. Combine the dry ingredients together in a small bowl (although I just do this in my measuring cup). Add them to the wet ingredients, whisking as you go, and then continue to whisk until it's smooth and thoroughly combined.

Pour the batter into the tin, scraping out the mixture with a spatula. Wriggle the cake a little to make the surface is even. Bake for 35–40 minutes and then check the cake with a skewer or toothpick. If it comes out clean, remove the cake from the oven. Lift the cake out of the tin and allow to cool.

Pour melted chocolate over the top, sprinkle with freeze-dried raspberries and then serve with runny coconut cream. Serious mouth-orgasm material.

CH-CH-CH-CH-CHANGES...

If you can't find dehydrated raspberries, use pistachios, pomegranate seeds or something else vibrant. You can also make this cake gluten-free by using a half/half blend of buckwheat and rice flour, and then adding a few extra tablespoons of buckwheat or coconut flour to thicken it a little.

SHOPPING LIST

For tht wet ingredients:
250 ml (8½ fl oz/1 cup) coconut milk (or your favorite non-dairy milk)
1 teaspoon apple cider vinegar
175 g (6 oz/¾ cup) granulated (raw) brown sugar (demerara)
75 ml (2½ fl oz/⅓ cup) coconut oil, melted
1 teaspoon vanilla extract
½ teaspoon almond extract (or 1 teaspoon if you really love almond)

For the dry ingredients:
125 g (4 oz/1 cup) plain (all-purpose) flour
60 g (2 oz/½ cup) cocoa powder
¾ teaspoon bicarbonate of soda (baking soda)
½ teaspoon baking powder
½ teaspoon sea salt

To decorate:
200g (7 oz/2 cups) vegan dark chocolate, chopped and melted
a handful of dehydrated raspberries
coconut milk, to serve

RHUBARB AND BERRY CRUMBLE

This recipe makes quite a lot of crumble topping, 'cos I'm a glutton like that. If you prefer a higher fruit to crumb ratio, halve the crumble recipe.

YOU NEED TO...

Preheat the oven to 180°C (350°F/Gas 4).

Chop the rhubarb and place in the bottom of a casserole dish with the berries (chop strawberries if using). Sprinkle the sugar on top and place the dish in the oven while you make the topping.

Combine all the topping ingredients in a bowl, working the syrup and coconut oil through with your fingers.

Remove the dish from the oven, stir once with a tablespoon and then sprinkle the topping on top of the fruit. Place the dish in the oven and bake for 45 minutes.

Allow to cool for 10 minutes before spooning into bowls and serving with Banana Ice Cream (see page 116) or Whipped Coconut Cream (see page 128).

CH-CH-CH-CH-CHANGES!

If you are gluten-free, use gluten-free oats. If you don't have any coconut oil you can use vegan margarine or even olive oil. Walnuts would work instead of almonds, ginger instead of cinnamon and, of course, you can use different fruit depending on what's in season.

SHOPPING LIST

For the fruit:
300 g (10½ oz) rhubarb
300 g (10½ oz/2 cups) berries
1 tablespoon granulated (raw) brown sugar (Demerara)

For the topping:
100 g (3½ oz/1 cup) rolled (porridge) oats
80 g (3 oz/½ cup) flaked almonds
40 g (1½ oz/½ cup) desiccated coconut
3 tablespoons coconut oil
3 tablespoons syrup sweetener, such as date, maple, golden or rice malt syrup
1 teaspoon vanilla powder or extract
1 teaspoon ground cinnamon
½ teaspoon sea salt

BANANA ICE CREAM

The secret to successful banana ice cream – or any banana treat, for that matter – is ripe and spotty bananas. As they age, bananas get sweeter and their texture more fluffy, giving you a sweet and fluffy ice cream that can then form the base for an array of different ice cream flavours. It's so easy and it never fails to blow people's minds!

YOU NEED TO...

Prep your bananas a night or two before you make the ice cream: peel and chop the bananas into chunks, then pop them into a plastic tub or freezer bag and place in the freezer until they have frozen.

Take the bananas out of the freezer and leave them to thaw for about 10 minutes so they aren't rock hard chunks.

Pop them into your food processor and blend until smooth and creamy. At first they will go almost crumbly, but the more you blend, the creamier they will get.

Add any of the optional extras you like and blend to combine, then serve or keep in the freezer until ready to eat!

TOP TIP

Once you get as addicted to this as I am, you will get into the habit of always having bananas ripening so you have at least a few ice-cream-ready bananas in your freezer.

SHOPPING LIST

2 spotty bananas

Optional extras:
1 teaspoon ground cinnamon
2 tablespoons peanut butter
1–2 tablespoons vegan chocolate chips
1 tablespoon maple syrup
2 tablespoons dehydrated strawberries
any other nut butter, sweetener or topping, depending on taste

BANANA BREAD

Banana bread has been in my life for as long as I can remember and it's one of the first recipes I veganised. It's the perfect way to use up bananas that have gone too spotty.

YOU NEED TO...

Preheat the oven to 180°C (350°F/Gas 4).

Peel the bananas and mash them in a large bowl. Add the rest of the ingredients, one at a time, in the order listed, stirring well between additions. When you get to the nuts, chocolate chips or coconut, add just over half to the batter.

Pour into a lined loaf tin or cake tin or some smaller tins. I use either a 23 x 10 cm (9 x 4 in) or a 28 x 10 cm (11 x 4 in) loaf tin. It works out well in both, though might need a slightly longer cooking time in the smaller pan. I also use a 20 cm (8 in) round cake tin if baking at the home of a friend who does not have a loaf tin. Top with the remaining nuts, chocolate chips or coconut.

Bake for 1 hour or until an inserted skewer comes out clean. If making muffins or lots of little loaves, they will need 30–40 minutes, cooking time.

NOTES

My favourite nuts to use are walnuts or pecans, but you can use anything you have on hand. You can even use a combination of flavours such as peanuts and chocolate chips.

SHOPPING LIST

4 ripe and spotty bananas

75 ml (2½ fl oz/⅓ cup) coconut oil, melted

1¼ teaspoons bicarbonate of soda (baking soda)

175 g (6 oz/¾ cup) granulated (raw) brown sugar (demerara)

185 g (6½ oz/1½ cups) plain (all-purpose) flour

a pinch of sea salt

1 teaspoon vanilla powder or extract (optional)

2 big handfuls of chopped nuts, vegan chocolate chips or desiccated coconut

THE KING

—

A vegan spin on the iconic Elvis sandwich of bacon, banana and peanut butter.

YOU NEED TO...

Place your frying pan (skillet) on a medium heat, melt some coconut oil in the bottom and place both slices of banana bread in there. When golden brown, flip and toast the other side (you can add more coconut oil before doing this if you wanna).

Slather some peanut butter on one slice of toasted bread, top with the coconut bacon, then the second slice of banana bread. Slice and eat!

NOTES

You can use a toaster or flat sandwich grill to toast the banana bread, but be careful putting super moist bread in the toaster as it might fall apart when you try to retrieve it – and we all hate losing things in the toaster, right? If you want extra decadence, add fresh bananas or melted vegan chocolate to the sandwich.

SHOPPING LIST

coconut oil
2 slices of Banana Bread (see page 117)
peanut butter
a handful of Coconut Bacon (see page 147)

VANILLA CHIA PUDDING

—

The always delicious, infinitely versatile and insanely simple vegan staple that also happens to be really, really good for you.

YOU NEED TO...

Combine the basic chia pudding ingredients in a 500 ml (17 fl oz/ 2 cups) jar. Screw on the lid and shake to combine. Shake again after 10 minutes to ensure no clumps are forming at the bottom (if they are, use a fork to separate them out). Place in the fridge overnight or for at least an hour.

Enjoy on its own or with any combination of fruit and nuts. If adding cacao powder, dissolve first with a tiny bit of hot water and then add to the milk before mixing in with the chia seeds. Some people like to add chocolate or peanut butter, but I prefer to keep the pudding itself simple.

Store in the fridge for up to a week.

TOP TIP

If you don't have a jar, you can use a bowl and fork — just make sure the mixture is really well stirred to prevent clumps from forming.

SHOPPING LIST

For the basic chia pudding:
2 tablespoons chia seeds
200 ml (7 fl oz/¾ cup) nut milk of your choice (coconut, almond, rice, oat, soy, hemp or a blend of your favourites)
1 tablespoon maple syrup
a pinch of sea salt
a splash of natural vanilla extract

Optional extras:
fruit, nuts, cacao powder

TANGY BERRY TARTS

—

A tangy lemon curd in a sweet and nutty crust, topped with fresh berries. These tarts are perfect as a morning, afternoon or evening treat on a hot summers day.

YOU NEED TO...

Either soak the cashew nuts overnight or boil in water for 15 minutes to soften. Rinse and drain. Line a 6-hole muffin tray or 6 separate moulds with individual squares of cling film (plastic wrap).

De-stone the dates and place in your food processor with the nuts. Pulse so that everything starts to break up. Add the cinnamon and salt, pulsing until the mixture comes together and can be moulded with your fingers.

Remove the mixture from the food processor and divide into 6 portions. Press these portions firmly into the lined moulds and then work them up the side of the moulds a little so that they form a little cup.

Wash and dry your food processor. Place the softened cashews, lemon juice and zest, maple syrup and vanilla in the food processor and blend until smooth.

Spoon the filling into the bases, using a rubber spatula to scrape off any extra mixture. Top with the berries, pressing them into the mixture a little so that they stay in place.

You can eat these immediately, but I prefer to pop them in the freezer for a couple of hours to set. Leave them in the freezer overnight if you wish, though they will then need a little thawing time, so you don't get brain freeze when you bite into them. If storing in the freezer for longer, remove from the moulds and pop them into an airtight container once they are hard.

SHOPPING LIST

155 g (5½ oz/1 cup) cashew nuts

For the bases:
5–7 Medjool dates
80 g (3 oz/½ cup) almonds
60 g (2 oz/½ cup) walnuts
½ teaspoon ground cinnamon
a pinch of sea salt

For the filling:
zest and juice of 2 lemons
2½ tablespoons maple syrup
½ teaspoon bourbon vanilla powder or vanilla extract
a couple of handfuls of your favourite fresh berries, to garnish

VEGAN GOODNESS

BLACK BEAN BROWNIE

When you break down the ingredients list, it's pretty much as healthy for you as making a really big banana, date and cacao smoothie for breakfast, and you add a tin of black beans as well. Add the fact that you are eating only one or two pieces at a time *ahem* and there really should be no guilt when consuming this, whether for breakfast, lunch, dinner, dessert or just as a good old-fashioned snack.

YOU NEED TO...

Preheat the oven to 180°C (350°F/Gas 4) and line a brownie tray (or casserole dish) with baking parchment.

Place everything, except the nuts, in your food processor and blend until smooth, scraping down the sides of the food processor as necessary. Roughly chop the nuts, add to the food processor and blend just to combine (you still want the nuts to be chunky).

Pour the mixture into your lined brownie tray, making sure you get all of the mix from under the blade of the food processor. Smooth down the mixture using the back of a spoon, then lick the spoon clean! Sprinkle the chopped pistachios, if using, and salt flakes on top.

Bake for 30 minutes. Allow to cool before cutting and eating (if you can). For that extra wow-factor, sprinkle over some edible flower petals.

SHOPPING LIST

3 spotty bananas, peeled

1 tin black beans or 250 g (9 oz/1½ cups) cooked black beans

6 Medjool dates, stones removed

125 g (4 oz/1 cup) cacao powder

60 g (2 oz/½ cup) buckwheat flour

2 teaspoons baking powder

50 ml (2 fl oz/¼ cup) coconut or olive oil

50 ml (2 fl oz/¼ cup) nut milk, water, orange juice or espresso

1 teaspoon natural vanilla extract

½ teaspoon salt

a large handful of pecans, walnuts or vegan chocolate chips

For the topping:

chopped pistachios or other nuts (optional)

sea salt flakes, to garnish

edible flower petals of your choice, to decorate

PEAR AND CARAMEL TART

Pears and caramel are a match made in heaven. You can serve this tart warm or cold.

YOU NEED TO...

Preheat the oven to 180°C (350°F/Gas 4).

To make the caramel, put the coconut milk in a small saucepan. Add the chopped dates to the pan and bring to the boil, then allow to simmer, whisking occasionally to help the dates break down. When the caramel is thick and smooth, remove from the heat, add the salt and vanilla powder (if using) and set aside.

To make the dough, place the flour, coconut oil, maple syrup and cinnamon (if using) in a bowl and mix with a fork until the ingredients are combined but the mixture is crumbly.

Add 50–100 ml (2–3½ fl oz/¼–⅓ cup) water, one tablespoon at a time, stirring between additions, until the mixture sticks together. Lightly knead into a ball in the bowl and then place the ball on a floured surface.

Press the ball into a circle with your fingertips. Flip and roll flat with a lightly floured rolling pin, then continue to flip and roll again, dusting the top with a little flour each time, until your crust is big enough to fit in your pie dish or cake tin and go up the side a little. If you are having difficulty rolling, let it rest a moment. Gently lift the dough into a pie dish or 23 cm (9 in) round springform cake tin.

Pour your prepared caramel into the crust. Place the scored pears on top and press down so they are nestled into the caramel. Sprinkle the chopped walnuts around the outer edge of the caramel. Bake for 40 minutes until nice and golden. Allow to cool for at least 10 minutes before serving with some Whipped Coconut Cream.

SHOPPING LIST

For the caramel:
400 ml (13 fl oz) tin coconut milk
10 Medjool dates, pits removed and finely chopped
a pinch of salt, plus more if needed
1 teaspoon vanilla powder (optional)

For the dough:
185 g (6½ oz/1½ cups) plain (all-purpose) flour, plus extra for rolling
50 ml (2 fl oz/¼ cup) coconut oil, melted
50 ml (2 fl oz/¼ cup) maple syrup
1 teaspoon ground cinnamon (optional)

For the topping:
3 pears, peeled, cut lengthwise and then finely scored the outside at 2 mm intervals - careful not to slice it all the way through (you want to create a beautiful lined pattern as pictured)
a handful of walnuts, roughly chopped
Whipped Coconut Cream (see page 128)

WHIPPED COCONUT CREAM

For when you need a lil' something cream-like to go with a cake or another sweet treat. This cream is so delicious with fresh fruit, chocolate and berries. You can even eat it on its own with a few seeds sprinkled on top – yum!

YOU NEED TO...

Gently scoop out the solidified coconut cream from the tin and place it in a mixing bowl. Reserve the remaining liquid and use in your smoothies.

Using an electric mixer or hand-held whisk, beat the coconut cream until it thickens, then add the sweetener and vanilla, if using, and beat some more until well combined.

Use immediately or store in the fridge until ready to use. It will keep in the fridge for 1–2 days.

NOTES

The brand of coconut milk I buy works perfectly every time I make this; however, I have read that some brands of coconut milk do not behave in a similar manner and that other brands sometimes do and sometimes don't. I have never had this problem but it is worth noting, in case you're wondering what the heck you have done wrong if this doesn't work out. It's not you, it's the coconuts. Where they grew up and how old they were when they were turned into coconut milk seem to play a part in their ability to cooperate.

If you don't have an electric mixer or hand-held whisk, unwhipped, runny, straight-up coconut milk is also a really yummy cream alternative.

SHOPPING LIST

2 x 400 ml (13 fl oz) tins coconut milk, refrigerated overnight, or coconut cream

1 tablespoon coconut nectar or maple syrup (optional)

1 teaspoon vanilla extract or cinnamon (optional)

LEMON AND POPPY SEED CAKE

——

Another one of my childhood favourites, veganised.

YOU NEED TO...

Preheat the oven to 180°C (350°F/Gas 4).

Finely grate the lemons to remove the zest and then juice them. Place the lemon zest, sugar, baking powder, bicarbonate of soda, vanilla, salt and 3 tablespoons of the poppy seeds in a large bowl and stir with a fork to combine.

Measure the lemon juice in a measuring jug. You should have 100–150 ml (3½–5 fl oz/about ½ cup) of juice. Add enough coconut milk to bring the liquid up to 350 ml (12 fl oz/1½ cups). Add the coconut oil to the cup. You should now have 400 ml (13 fl oz/1¾ cups) of liquid.

Pour the liquid into the large bowl with the other ingredients and whisk to combine. The combination of bicarbonate of soda and the citrus juices will have a foaming effect that gives the cake its airy lightness. Add the flour to the bowl and whisk until the mixture is smooth.

Pour the mixture into a 28 cm (11 in) loaf tin lined with baking parchment and sprinkle a thick layer of the remaining poppy seeds over the top.

Bake for 45 minutes or until an inserted skewer comes out clean.

CH-CH-CH-CH-CHANGES...

You can use any citrus fruit in place of the lemons, such as 2 oranges or 4 limes, or a mixture of all three.

SHOPPING LIST

3 organic lemons (you're using zest in the cake so best to use organic if possible)

175 g (6 oz/¾ cup) granulated (raw) brown sugar (demerara)

1 teaspoon baking powder

1 teaspoon bicarbonate of soda (baking soda)

1 teaspoon vanilla powder or natural vanilla extract

½ teaspoon sea salt

6 tablespoons poppy seeds

250 ml (8½ fl oz/1 cup) coconut milk

50 ml (2 fl oz/¼ cup) coconut oil, melted

310 g (11 oz/2½ cups) plain (all-purpose) flour

SUPER PORRIDGE

The perfect breakfast or sweet snack that will warm your insides and make your skin glow.

YOU NEED TO...

Place the rice flakes or quinoa, coconut milk and 250 ml (8½ fl oz/1 cup) of water in a small saucepan on a high heat and bring to a boil.

Once boiling, lower to a medium heat and allow to simmer away until all of the liquid is absorbed – about 5 minutes, but keep an eye on it.

Stir in the cinnamon, salt, vanilla and blueberries.

Spoon into bowls and top with your favourite antioxidant-filled foods. Pictured here are hemp seeds, pomegranate seeds, coconut flakes, pumpkin seeds, coconut sugar and a dollop of coconut cream.

CH-CH-CH-CH-CHANGES...

You can use standard oats or buckwheat in place of rice or quinoa flakes. Use raspberries or blackberries if you can't find blueberries.

SHOPPING LIST

100 g (3½ oz/1 cup) rice flakes or quinoa flakes

250 ml (8½ fl oz/1 cup) coconut milk

2 teaspoons ground cinnamon

a pinch of sea salt

½ teaspoon vanilla powder or extract (optional)

150 g (5 oz/1 cup) blueberries

To serve (optional):
hemp seeds
pomegranate seeds
coconut flakes
pumpkin seeds
coconut sugar
coconut cream

CONDIMENTS
AND DRINKS

—

GREEN PESTO

When I first became vegan I feared that pesto would never be the same without Parmesan, but I can truly, honestly say I do not miss it. There is so much flavour from the herbs, nuts and salt that you don't even notice the lack of cheese. Trust me! This is one of those recipes that I never, ever measure and very rarely make the same twice. I just chuck everything in the food processor and blend it until I am happy with the consistency. I usually make a double batch and freeze half in two separate containers for lazy Sunday pasta dinners.

YOU NEED TO...

Remove the large stalks from the basil and parsley and roughly chop the leaves and finer stalks. Place them in a food processor.

Roughly chop the garlic and add to the food processor along with the lemon juice, olive oil, salt and some freshly ground black pepper. Blend until well combined. I like a thick pesto. If you would like a more runny pesto, add more oil.

Add the nuts and blend until finely chopped. Use immediately or store in an airtight jar until ready to use. It will keep in the fridge for up to a week.

CH-CH-CH-CH-CHANGES...

Instead of pine nuts, a combination of pumpkin and sunflower seeds also works well, as do walnuts. To get a really creamy pesto, you can substitute the olive oil an avocado. It is insanely delicious, and the lemon juice will keep it fresh for a couple of days, but it is best eaten on the day if doing this.

SHOPPING LIST

a big bunch of basil

a big bunch of parsley

2–3 garlic cloves, peeled

juice of 1 lemon

a large drizzle of olive oil (about 75 ml/2½ fl oz/⅓ cup)

½ teaspoon sea salt

freshly ground black pepper, to taste

a large handful of toasted pine nuts or cashews

FRESH TOMATO NAPOLI SAUCE

——

This sauce is a key ingredient in my Lasagne on page 67, Spag Bol with Courgette Zoodles on page 36 and Rollatini on page 76 or you can also use it on its own over cooked pasta noodles for a quick after-work meal.

YOU NEED TO...

Pour a little olive oil into a medium-sized saucepan and place on a medium heat.

Finely chop the shallots and garlic and add to the pan. Dice the tomatoes into small cubes and add these to the pan, including the seeds and juices.

Slice the olive flesh away from the olive stones and then chop a little more so you have lots of little pieces of olive. Add to the pan. You can use olives without their stones if you like, but their flavour is not as authentic.

Stir the tomato paste into the sauce and allow it to simmer away on a medium-low heat for 10 minutes. Finely chop the parsley and add to the sauce, then season to taste.

CH-CH-CH-CH-CHANGES...

You can add mushrooms, aubergine (eggplant) or courgette (zucchini) if you want a slightly more hearty sauce. Basil leaves also make a great addition. You can use tinned tomatoes if it's not tomato season or you can't be bothered with all the chopping.

SHOPPING LIST

olive oil

2 shallots, peeled

3–5 garlic cloves, peeled

about 1 kg (2 lb 3 oz) tomatoes (I use a combination of normal and cherry)

10–20 black olives

1 tablespoon tomato paste (concentrated purée)

a handful of flat-leaf (Italian) parsley

sea salt and freshly ground black pepper

MUSHROOM GRAVY

Seriously the best gravy you will ever try. Enjoy with the Nut Roast on page 71 with roasted potatoes or drizzled on top of a big bowl of roasted, mashed veggies.

YOU NEED TO...

Soak the mushrooms in 250 ml (8½ fl oz/1 cup) of water for at least 1 hour. Drain, reserving the water, then finely chop the mushrooms.

Heat a glug of olive oil in a medium-sized frying pan (skillet) and add the finely chopped onion or shallot. Cook until clear, then add the white wine or vermouth and veggie stock and whisk in the flour and nutmeg.

Add the reserved water to the pan with the garlic and soaked mushrooms. Allow to simmer and thicken for 10–15 minutes.

Season generously with freshly ground black pepper and then taste. Add salt until the flavour pops (the amount you need will depend on the saltiness of the veggie stock you used).

SHOPPING LIST

20 g (¾ oz/1 cup) dried mushrooms
olive oil

1 small white onion or shallot, peeled and finely chopped

2 tablespoons dry white wine or vermouth

250 ml (8½ fl oz/1 cup) vegetable stock

3 tablespoons plain (all-purpose) flour, to thicken

½ teaspoon ground nutmeg

2 garlic cloves, peeled and finely chopped

sea salt and freshly ground black pepper

ODE TO CASHEWS

—

Have you seen how cashew nuts grow? They grow on a tree and each cashew nut is the seed of a cashew apple. The nuts grow on the outside of the fleshy fruit and to get to the nut, workers have to break through two layers of highly toxic hard shell, which wreaks havoc on their hands and can also ruin the nut that is nestled inside. It is one of those incredible creations of Mother Nature that blows my mind. I mean, who was the first person to break through those two layers of nut shell to find the nut inside? And then, after the shell made the nut go rancid, using different methods to figure out the best way to extract the nut without destroying it?

Besides eating them toasted or raw, throwing a handful in a curry, stir fry or salad, or popping a few into my smoothies, two of my favourite things to make with them are Cashew Cream and Chipotle Mayo. They also make a great substitute for cream cheese in cheesecakes.

CASHEW CREAM

YOU NEED TO...

Either soak the nuts overnight in a bowl or jug filled with water or boil them in a small saucepan filled with water for about 15 minutes. Most cashews have already been heat-treated when they get to you, so this isn't going to render them 'no longer raw' – they weren't raw to begin with.

Strain and rinse the nuts, then place them in a blending receptacle and add enough water so that the nuts are just covered (it's fine if there are a few bits sticking out the top).

Blend until smooth. If you require a runnier consistency, add a little more water. Store in an airtight container and keep chilled until ready to use. It will keep in the fridge for up to a week.

SHOPPING LIST

100 g (3½ oz/⅔ cup) cashew nuts

CHIPOTLE MAYO

YOU NEED TO...

Crush the garlic and add to the Cashew Cream along with the lemon juice, chipotle, mustard, salt and some freshly ground black pepper. Blend to combine.

Taste. If it lacks punch, add more salt. Store in an airtight container and keep chilled until ready to use. It will keep in the fridge for up to a week.

SHOPPING LIST

2–3 garlic cloves, peeled

250 ml (8½ fl oz/1 cup) Cashew Cream (see recipe opposite)

juice of ½ lemon

1 teaspoon ground dried chipotle peppers or smoked paprika

⅓–¾ teaspoon mustard

½ teaspoon sea salt

freshly ground black pepper

BLUEBERRY AND CHIA JAM

—

The quickest, easiest, healthiest jam you will ever make.

YOU NEED TO...

Place the berries and maple syrup in a small saucepan and mash together with a fork or the back of a spoon. Place the saucepan over a medium heat and simmer for 10 minutes.

Stir in the chia seeds, vanilla extract and cinnamon and allow to cool. The jam will thicken as it cools. Transfer to an airtight jar until ready to serve. This can be stored in the fridge for up to a week.

IT'S DELICIOUS ON...

Fig and walnut bread. Like, get-the-hell-outta-town delicious. Also makes a great topping for a cheesecake or another cake.

SHOPPING LIST

310 g (11 oz/2 cups) fresh or frozen blueberries, raspberries or blackberries

2 tablespoons maple syrup or any other sweetener of your choice (sugar, honey)

2 tablespoons chia seeds

½ teaspoon natural vanilla extract

1 teaspoon ground cinnamon

SAUCES AND DRESSINGS

Use these measurements as a guide only. I usually eyeball it or use the same tablespoon that I am mixing everything with (which holds about 15 ml/½ fl oz), rather than getting all fiddly with measuring cups and spoons and what not.

CREAMY TAHINI DRESSING

SHOPPING LIST

juice of 1–2 lemons
60 ml (2 fl oz/¼ cup) tahini
a splash of balsamic vinegar
sea salt and freshly ground black pepper

YOU NEED TO...

In a bowl, combine the lemon juice, tahini, balsamic and a little water. Stir to combine. It will go really thick at first, but will thin out as you add water. Keep adding water, little by little, until it is smooth and liquid-like in consistency. Season to taste. Decant into a clean jar. It will keep in the fridge for up to a week.

Depending on what you are using this with, you might need to sweeten it. I usually make this for my Coleslaw (see page 82), which contains apple, and they are divine together!

BASIC BALSAMIC VINAIGRETTE

SHOPPING LIST

120 ml (4 fl oz/½ cup) olive oil
3 tablespoons balsamic vinegar
2 teaspoons mustard
sea salt and freshly ground black pepper

YOU NEED TO...

Place everything together in a bottle or glass jar, put the lid on and shake. The mustard will act as an emulsifier and help the oil and liquid to stay together. You can add salt and pepper if you like, but I prefer to add this directly to my salad. It will keep at room temperature for 2–3 weeks.

Serve over any basic green side salad, Greek salad, bean salad or a heartier salad that contains greens, beans and other veggies.

SATAY SAUCE

SHOPPING LIST

125 g (4 oz/½ cup) smooth peanut butter
60 ml (2 fl oz/¼ cup) tamari or soy sauce
60 ml (2 fl oz/¼ cup) maple syrup
or any other liquid sweetener

YOU NEED TO...

Combine the peanut butter, tamari and maple syrup
and stir vigorously until they form a thick, brown
sauce. Add some water little by little, stirring between
additions, until it reaches a consistency you like. I use
about 2 tablespoons, but the amount you need will
ultimately depend on the thickness of your peanut
butter. Don't worry if you are unsure exactly how
thick to make it. Once it's all over a bowl of warm
veggies, it tastes delicious and that's all that matters.
Also makes a great dunking sauce for rice paper rolls.

PEANUT SAUCE

SHOPPING LIST

Exactly the same as the Satay Sauce, minus the tamari.
Delicious with Falafel (see page 58).

MAPLE LIME DRESSING

SHOPPING LIST

juice of 1–2 limes
1–2 tablespoons maple syrup or any other liquid sweetener
1 tablespoon toasted sesame or peanut oil
tamari or soy sauce, to taste

YOU NEED TO...

Squeeze the lime juice into some kind of vessel. Add
the maple syrup, sesame oil and a teaspoon of tamari.
Stir and taste. Add additional tamari if you need it
saltier or additional maple if you need it sweeter. Serve
over a noodle salad such as my Summer Roll Salad (see
page 52) or anything with strong flavours that requires
a sweet, fresh, light dressing.

STRAIGHT UP LEMON JUICE

Sometimes that's all a salad needs. No oil, no salt,
just a bit of tang to bring out the flavours of the other
ingredients. Try it!

COCONUT BACON

Legend has it that this idea arose from vegan punks pouring liquid smoke onto fresh baby coconuts and calling it bacon. The idea caught on and now coconut bacon is something of a staple amongst vegans and vegetarians. Thank you, punks. We owe you one!

YOU NEED TO...

Preheat the oven to 180°C (350°F/Gas 4).

Mix the liquid smoke, maple syrup, tamari and 1 tablespoon of water in a medium-sized bowl. Add the coconut flakes and gently stir with a tablespoon until they are coated in the liquid mix.

Spread the coconut flakes on a baking tray and place in the oven for 5 minutes. Remove the tray, stir and flip the flakes with a metal spatula and then return to the oven for another 5 minutes, keeping an eye (or nose, rather) on it to ensure the flakes do not burn.

After the second 5 minutes, the flakes should be golden and crispy, but if they are still a bit white and soft, return them to the oven for another few minutes. Transfer the coconut flakes to a plate and allow to cool there (or they will continue to cook on the hot baking tray).

When entirely cool, store in an airtight container, until ready to eat. Coconut bacon keeps well in the freezer for several months. No need to defrost! At room temperature, it will keep for 1–2 weeks

IT'S DELICIOUS ON...

The King (see page 118) or in a sandwich, bagel, burger or wrap; on top of pizza, on top of pancakes, on ice cream; in burgers and salads; or straight out of the jar. You get the gist.

SHOPPING LIST

2 tablespoons liquid smoke

2 tablespoons maple syrup (or coconut nectar if this is available to you)

1 tablespoon tamari or soy sauce

100 g (3½ oz/2 cups) coconut flakes (not desiccated coconut)

CARAMELISED ONIONS

Caramelised onions have the ability to transform any dish from OK to gourmet. They take time, but don't need much attention, so you can pop them on and let them do their thing while you prep the remainder of the feast.

YOU NEED TO...

Pour enough olive oil into a frying pan (skillet) to cover the base and place the pan on a low–medium heat.

Chop the onions in half, remove the skin and then chop each half into 5 mm (¼ in) slices or 8 wedges. Don't cut them too thin or they will go dry and burnt before they are ready.

Place the onion slices in the pan and let them slowly soften and caramelise while you go about other cooking duties in your kitchen, stirring them every 5–10 minutes to prevent sticking and to coat them in their own juices. They will go soft and translucent first and then slowly turn to an irresistible brown colour with a smell so incredible you won't be able to resist eating one from the pan, even though it will burn the roof of your mouth.

When they look done, add the balsamic vinegar and some salt and allow to cook for another 5 minutes.

Use immediately, or allow to cool and then transfer to an airtight jar where they will remain good for up to a week.

CHEATING

Low and slow is best, but some people don't have the time or patience for this. If you want to, you can add a couple of tablespoons of brown sugar or maple syrup. This will add to the caramel flavour, but shorten the cooking time.

SHOPPING LIST

olive oil
3 large onions (white or red)
1–2 tablespoons balsamic vinegar
sea salt, to taste

SERVES 4, DEPENDING ON THE SIZE OF YOUR MELON

WATERMELON LIMEADE

—

Here's the thing about watermelons. They're great. They are tasty as heck and on top of that, really, really good for you. But taking them out of the house can be damn messy. Messy is fine if you're picnicking alongside a body of water. Not so fine if you're at the park.

My solution? Bottled watermelon.

YOU NEED TO...

Place the flat end of the melon half on your chopping board and remove the skin in downward slices. Keeping the flat end of the melon on the board, slice the melon as you would a loaf of bread.

Pick up a slice of melon and you will see the seeds are clustered in a line. Using your hands, gently break the melon along this line. Scrape the seeds off with a spoon and then place the seedless flesh in your blending receptacle. Repeat until you have done this with all of the slices.

That's it. Turn on your blending device and blend the chunks of melon until they are smooth. Add the juice of your fresh lime or limes and blend once more to combine.

Pour into glasses with ice and mint or store in the fridge until ready to drink. If doing this, you will need to give it a swirl before you drink it.

CH-CH-CH-CH-CHANGES...

Turn it into a cocktail by adding vodka, tequila, gin or white rum!

SHOPPING LIST

½ large watermelon
1–3 limes
ice cubes, to serve
mint, to garnish (optional)

BANANA-BASED SMOOTHIES

—

Everyone is all about green smoothies these days, but I still love a good old fashioned banana smoothie that is so decadent you could drink it as a dessert as well as for breakfast.

The method is the same for all of the recipes here: place everything in a blending receptacle and blend until well combined.

Clockwise from top: Turmeric; Cacao Nib; Blueberry Blackberry; Raspberry Orange; Matcha Peanut Butter; Peanut Butter; Cherry Coconut

PEANUT BUTTER

SHOPPING LIST

2 bananas
150 ml (5 fl oz/⅔ cup) rice milk
2 tablespoons peanut butter

TURMERIC

SHOPPING LIST

2 bananas
200 ml (7 fl oz/1 cup) nut milk of your choice
½ teaspoon ground turmeric
½ teaspoon ground cinnamon

CHERRY COCONUT

SHOPPING LIST

2 bananas
a large handful of cherries, pitted
150 ml (5 fl oz/⅔ cup) coconut milk

BLUEBERRY BLACKBERRY

SHOPPING LIST

2 bananas
a small handful of blueberries
a small handful of blackberries
150 ml (5 fl oz/⅔ cup) coconut water

RASPBERRY ORANGE

SHOPPING LIST

2 bananas
juice of 2 oranges
a handful of raspberries

MATCHA

SHOPPING LIST

2 bananas
200 ml (7 fl oz/1 cup) almond milk
2 teaspoons matcha powder, dissolved in a little hot water

CACAO NIB

SHOPPING LIST

2 bananas
200 ml (7 fl oz/1 cup) coconut milk
1 tablespoon cacao nibs

OPTIONAL EXTRAS

— chia seeds, soaked in the liquid you are using
— 1–2 tablespoons quick (porridge) oats
— 1 teaspoon ground cinnamon
— hemp seeds
— desiccated coconut
— almond flakes

GINGER TURMERIC TONIC

—

I drink this even when I am not sick because it is just so damn good for you.

YOU NEED TO...

Wearing gloves so that you don't stain your hands and look like you have smoked 50 packets of cigarettes in one sitting, remove the skins from the ginger and turmeric using the edge of a teaspoon, scraping against the growth pattern. When most of the skin is off, chop roughly.

Juice the lemons and put the chopped ginger, turmeric, lemon juice, cayenne pepper and syrup in a blending receptacle. Blend until well combined. You may need to get some chunky bits of ginger off your blade every once in a while. Store in an airtight glass jar, in the fridge, until ready to use.

To use, mix 1 heaped teaspoon into a cup of water. You can use boiling water, warm water or sparkling water if you wish, to turn this into a healthy lemonade. Add more sweetener of choice to taste. Drink.

NOTES

There will be some chunky bits left in the bottom of the cup. Think of these like 'tea leaves'. You can eat them if you want to, or pop them in the compost if the drink was intense enough for you.

SHOPPING LIST

100 g (3½oz) fresh ginger
100 g (3½ oz) fresh turmeric
6 lemons
1 teaspoon cayenne pepper
3 tablespoons rice malt syrup or maple syrup

THANK YOUS

—

Andy – they say behind every great man there is a great woman. In my case the opposite applies. From the last-minute supermarket trips for forgotten ingredients, to cleaning the kitchen just so I can mess it up again, taking notes, ironing backdrops, holding tripods, listening to me talk about nothing but this damn book for days on end and for making me a kick ass playlist to keep me bopping when morale was low. This is not *my* book, it's *our* book, because I could not have done it without you. I love you.

My mum, for instilling me with my love for cooking.

My friends, for your honesty through all of my recipe tweaking, the back rubs after days on end of shooting with a pregnant belly, for helping me eat three–day-old food so I didn't have to waste it and for cooking for me when I couldn't bear the thought of my own cooking anymore.

Hannah, for creating most of the pottery I used in my photos. Your creations made my book ten times more beautiful than it would have been without them. www.jerichostudiopottery.com

Astrid, for the photos that I couldn't take myself.

Helly, for being my trusty Kiwi sidekick in those months when I could only just see my toes.

Kajal, Kate and the team at Hardie Grant for believing in me and letting me make this book.

Michelle, for your illustrations and for doing such a beautiful job with the design.

And finally, a big thank you to the cooks of the world, whether I have tasted your food or not. Thank you for sharing your food, your recipes and your ideas. Without you all, I would not have this book.

ABOUT JESSICA

—

Jessica Prescott is the writer and photographer behind the stylish vegan blog *Wholy Goodness* (www.wholygoodness.com) which was nominated as a finalist in the Best New Voice category in the Saveur awards. She grew up in Napier – the fruit bowl of New Zealand – and now lives in Berlin.

Wholy Goodness is a manifestation of her long-held desire to share her kitchen experiments. It is also a space where she can combine all of her creative outlets – food, photography and hand lettering. @wholygoodness

INDEX

VEGAN GOODNESS

First published in 2016 by Hardie Grant Books, an imprint of
Hardie Grant Publishing

Hardie Grant Books (UK)
52–54 Southwark Street
London SE1 1UN

Hardie Grant Books (Australia)
Ground Floor, Building 1
658 Church Street
Melbourne, VIC 3121

hardiegrantbooks.com

The moral rights of Jessica Prescott to be identified as the
author of this work have been asserted by her in accordance
with the Copyright, Designs and Patents Act 1988.

Text © Jessica Prescott
Photography © Jessica Prescott

All rights reserved. No part of this publication may be reproduced,
stored in a retrieval system or transmitted in any form by any
means, electronic, electrostatic, magnetic tape, mechanical,
photocopying, recording or otherwise, without the prior written
permission of the Publisher.

British Library Cataloguing-in-Publication Data. A catalogue record
for this book is available from the British Library.

ISBN: 978-1-78488-047-7

Publisher: Kate Pollard
Senior Editor: Kajal Mistry
Editorial Assistant: Hannah Roberts
Photographer: Jessica Prescott
Art Direction and Illustrations: Michelle Noel
Copy editor: Kay Delves
Proofreader: Charlotte Coleman-Smith
Indexer: Cathy Heath
Retouchers: Butterfly Creative Services and Steve McCabe
Colour Reproduction by p2d

Printed and bound in China by Toppan Leefung

BEDTIME LULLABY

KU-166-757

This book belongs to:

....

Twinkle Twinkle, Little Star

Twinkle twinkle, little star,
How I wonder what you are.
Up above the world so high,
Like a diamond in the sky.
Twinkle twinkle, little star,
How I wonder what you are.

Rock-a-bye Baby

Rock-a-bye baby, in the treetop.

When the wind blows, the cradle will rock,

When the bough breaks, the cradle will fall,

Down will come baby, cradle and all.

Come to the Window

Come to the window,
My baby, with me,
And look at the stars
That shine on the sea.
There are two little stars
That play bo-peep,
With two little fish
Far down in the deep;
And two little frogs
Cry, "Neap, neap, neap";
I see a dear baby
That should be asleep.

Where Should a Baby Rest?

Where should a baby rest?
Where but on its mother's arm.
Where can a baby lie
Half so safe from every harm?
Lulla, lulla, lullaby,
Softly sleep my baby.
Lulla, lulla, lullaby,
Soft, soft my baby.

Nestle there, my lovely one,
Press to mine thy velvet cheek.
Sweetly coo, and smile, and look,
All the love thou canst not speak.
Lulla, lulla, lullaby,
Softly sleep my baby.
Lulla, lulla, lullaby,
Soft, soft my baby.

Lavender's Blue

Lavender's blue, dilly, dilly,
Lavender's green;
When you are King, dilly, dilly,
I shall be Queen.

Call up your friends, dilly, dilly,
Set them to work;
Some to the plough, dilly, dilly,
Some to the fork.

Some to make hay, dilly, dilly,
Some to thresh corn;
While you and I, dilly, dilly,
Keep ourselves warm.

Lavender's blue, dilly, dilly,
Lavender's green;
When I am King, dilly, dilly,
You shall be Queen.

Hush Little Baby

Hush little baby, don't say a word,
Papa's gonna buy you a mockingbird.
If that mockingbird don't sing,
Papa's gonna buy you a diamond ring.

If that diamond ring turns to brass,
Papa's gonna buy you a looking glass.
If that looking glass gets broke,
Papa's gonna buy you a billy goat.

If that billy goat won't pull,

Papa's gonna buy you a cart and bull.

If that cart and bull turn over,

Papa's gonna buy you a dog named Rover.

If that dog named Rover won't bark,

Papa's gonna buy you a horse and cart.

If that horse and cart fall down,

You'll be the sweetest little baby in town.

Star Light, Star Bright

Star light, star bright,

First star I see tonight.

I wish I may, I wish I might,

Have the wish I wish tonight.

Bye, Baby Bunting

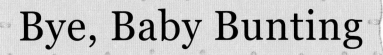

Bye, baby bunting,

Daddy's gone a-hunting,

A rosy wisp of cloud to win

To wrap the baby bunting in.

Bye, baby bunting.

Brahms' Lullaby

Lullaby and good night,
In the sky stars are bright.
'Round your head flowers gay
Scent your slumber till day.

Close your eyes now and rest,
May these hours be blessed.
Go to sleep now and rest
May your slumber be blessed.

Frère Jacques

Frère Jacques, Frère Jacques,

Dormez-vous? Dormez-vous?

Sonnez les matines,

Sonnez les matines,

Din, din, don. Din, din, don.

Are you sleeping, are you sleeping?

Brother John? Brother John?

Morning bells are ringing,

Morning bells are ringing,

Ding, ding, dong. Ding, ding, dong.

The Man in the Moon

The man in the Moon
Looked out of the Moon
And this is what he said:
"'Tis time for all children on the Earth
To think about getting to bed."

Matthew, Mark, Luke and John

Matthew, Mark, Luke and John,

Bless the bed that I lie on.

Four corners to my bed,

Four angels 'round my head.

One to watch and one to pray

And two to bear my soul away.

Rocking Carol

Little baby, sweetly sleep, do not stir,
We will lend a coat of fur.

We will rock you, rock you, rock you,
We will rock you, rock you, rock you.

See the fur to keep you warm,
Gently round your tiny form.

Precious little baby, sleep, sweetly sleep,
Sleep in comfort, slumber deep.

We will rock you, rock you, rock you,
We will rock you, rock you, rock you.

Little baby, do not cry,
We will sing a lullaby.

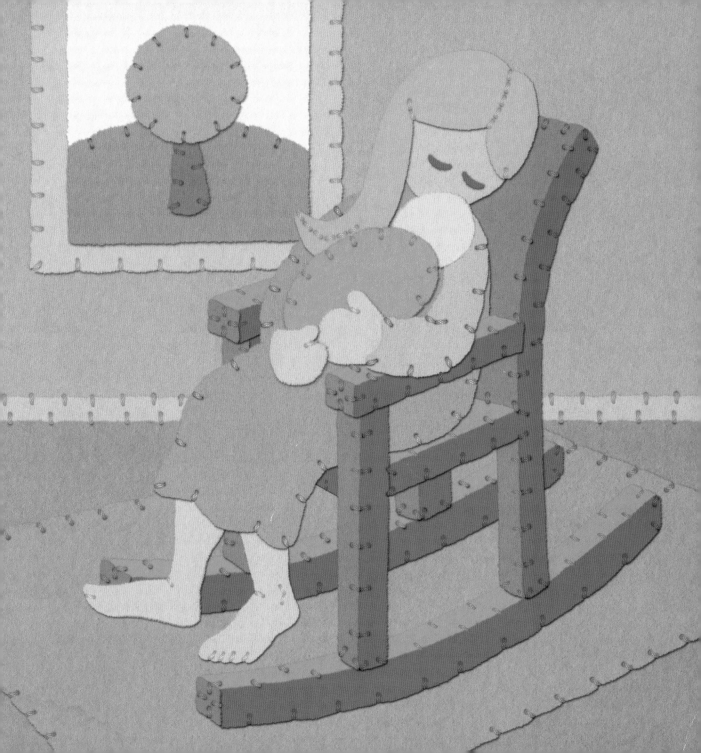

Sleep, Baby, Sleep

Sleep, baby, sleep,
Your father guards the sheep.
Your mother shakes the dreamland tree
And from it fall sweet dreams for thee.
Sleep, baby, sleep.

Sleep, baby, sleep,
Our cottage vale is deep.
The little lamb is on the green,
With snowy fleece so soft and clean.
Sleep, baby, sleep.

Sleep, baby, sleep,
Down where the woodbines creep.
Be always like the lamb so mild,
A kind, and sweet, and gentle child.
Sleep, baby, sleep.

Winkum, Winkum

Winkum, winkum, shut your eyes
While I sing sweet lullabies;
For the dews are falling soft,
Lights are flick'ring up aloft;
And the moonlight's peeping over
Yonder hilltop capped with clover.

Chickens long have gone to rest,
Birds lie snug within their nest.
And my darling soon will be
Sleeping like a chickadee.
For with only half a try,
Winkum, winkum shuts her eyes.

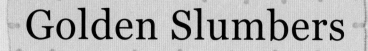

Golden Slumbers

Golden slumbers kiss your eyes,

Smiles await you when you rise.

Sleep, pretty baby, do not cry,

And I will sing a lullaby.

Care you know not, therefore sleep,
While I o'er you watch do keep.
Sleep, pretty baby, do not cry,
And I will sing a lullaby.